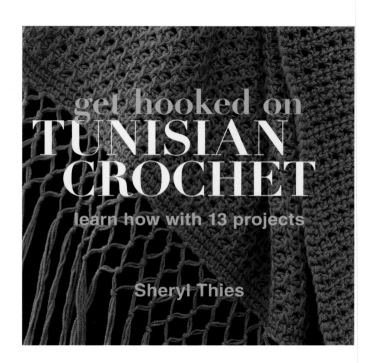

get hooked on
TUNISIAN
CROCHET

learn how with 13 projects

Sheryl Thies

Martingale®
& COMPANY

Get Hooked on Tunisian Crochet:
Learn How with 13 Projects
© 2011 by Sheryl Thies

Martingale & Company®
19021 120th Ave. NE, Suite 102
Bothell, WA 98011-9511 USA
www.martingale-pub.com

Printed in China
16 15 14 13 12 11   8 7 6 5 4 3 2 1

Credits

President & CEO—Tom Wierzbicki

Editorial Director—Mary V. Green

Managing Editor—Tina Cook

Technical Editor—Ursula Reikes

Copy Editor—Liz McGehee

Design Director—Stan Green

Production Manager—Regina Girard

Illustrator—Laurel Strand

Cover & Text Designer—Shelly Garrison

Photographer—Brent Kane

Special thanks to Pam and Darrel
Coney, Woodniville, Washington for
generously allowing us to photograph
in their beautiful yard.

Mission Statement

Dedicated to providing quality products
and service to inspire creativity.

**Library of Congress Cataloging-in-Publication
Data is available upon request.**

ISBN: 978-1-60468-035-5

DEDICATION

To Coda—your delight and
determination to learn
and develop inspires me.

ACKNOWLEDGMENTS

Sometimes things just fall into place,
especially with a little help along
the way. And for this publication
things went smoothly, thanks to
my many friends. My gratitude
goes to Linda Krag, with Denise
Interchangeable Needles, who was
the first to encourage me to design
and publish my Tunisian crochet
work. Ursula and Ruth lent their
hands to work up projects; for that I
am extremely grateful. Ladies, thank
you, your work is flawless. Thanks
to Jac, Jackie, Ellie, Sara, and many
others for the creative times spent
together offering honest critiques,
suggestions, and thoughts and for
forcing me to stretch and expand
my thinking. A special thanks goes
to Mary Green and the entire
Martingale staff, who worked their
magic to spin my manuscript into this
book. I'm indebted to Ursula Reikes,
my technical editor; her persistence
and care clarified, corrected, and
improved my initial work. And last
but not least, thanks to my husband,
Kevin, who often made reservations
for dinner.

CONTENTS

intersection of
TECHNIQUE and FIBER

Walking through the aisles of vendors at The National Needlearts Association (TNNA) trade show, surrounded by the miles of yarn, buttons, and pins; a vast selection of bags; racks of books, hooks, and needles; and other accessories can be overwhelming and awe-inspiring. As I approached an intersection of aisles, I spied a young woman with a beautifully textured, multicolored afghan unfolding over her lap, feverishly working with an enormous wooden implement; she had a hook with a wire tail in one hand and in the other she held a bunch of yarn strands emanating from a tangle of yarns spilling out of an unzipped gym bag at her feet. Mesmerized, I watched as she swiftly worked across and back without ever turning her work, the afghan growing with each row.

This introduction to Tunisian crochet was graciously given by Jennifer Hansen, aka Stitch Diva, as she worked on one of her Tunisian Stash Buster Blankets. Before she finished the brief demonstration of the basics, I knew I wanted to become proficient in the technique. The smooth rhythm of the forward and return passes, the wonderful textured fabric, and the visible progress that each row added appealed to me.

With the help of needlework books from the 1960s and '70s (the last time Tunisian crochet was popular), and a little practice, I quickly mastered the basics. The stitches were simple and quick to work, yet the fabric looked intricate and complex. Traditionally, the resulting fabric is dense, thick, and sturdy, suitable for winter wear and rugs; but by using larger hooks and newer yarns, some with a surprising combination of fibers, the fabric can be soft, supple, and open.

Relying on my knitting and design knowledge, I began to experiment with hooks, yarn, and stitches. Many of the textures and designs were pleasantly pleasing. The result of my experimentation—this book—includes an illustrated tutorial for learning Tunisian crochet, as well as complete instructions for creating distinctive and unique designs.

If you are already familiar with the basics of Tunisian crochet, you may want to jump right in with a project that has a unique stitch pattern or a project that requires shaping. If you are just learning, don't be shy about moving on to a project that incorporates a stitch pattern. Feel free to create a one-of-a-kind look by adding your own personal touch.

When technique intersects with fiber, the results can sometimes be unanticipated. But beware; you just may get hooked.

—Sheryl

A Rose
by Any Other Name

When Juliet whispered to Romeo that a name is artificial and meaningless, she easily could have been speaking about Tunisian crochet rather than her ill-fated and tragic love affair. Tunisian crochet, afghan stitch, *tricoter à la crochet*, princess royal stitch, princess Fredrick William stitch, shepherd's knitting, railway stitch, idiot stitch, and fool's stitch are a sampling of names used to define the technique.

Tunisian crochet, or whatever term you prefer, is worked with a long crochet hook that looks similar to a knitting needle, but with a hook on one end and a button-type stopper at the other end. The stitches are worked on a foundation of crochet chains in two passes. The first or forward pass, worked from right to left across the row, picks up and keeps the stitches on the hook, creating the vertical strand of the stitch. The return pass, worked from left to right across the row, removes the stitches from the hook and creates the horizontal strand of the stitch. The forward and return passes make up one row.

Knitting and weaving have a long and well-documented history, while crochet and Tunisian crochet seem to be more recent crafts. Crochet, named after a French word for small hook, emerged in the mid-1800s in England as a new invention. No obvious link to Tunisia, the northernmost country in Africa, seems to exist, even though Tunisia is known for its wool trade and other textiles. Although Tunisian crochet may have existed elsewhere in the world at an earlier time, very little documented history exists; perhaps some future discovery will provide the missing pieces of the story.

Some sources suggest this technique is a cross between knitting and crocheting and even hint that because such a simple tool (the hook) is used, it may be the forerunner of both knitting and crocheting. A Tunisian crochet hook looks somewhat like a knitting needle, and some stitches look similar to knitted fabric, but beyond that there are few similarities. Rather than a cross between knitting and crocheting, Tunisian crochet is probably more accurately considered a subset of crochet.

Penelope, a women's magazine published in Holland between 1821 and 1833, first included crochet patterns in 1824. In many cases only the stitch pattern and a diagram were given. The needle worker was expected to learn the stitch pattern, and then follow the diagram to complete the piece, rather than follow line-by-line directions.

In Germany during the 1840s, women's craft magazines proliferated, and crochet became a mainstream craft. It's at this point in history that Tunisian crochet, as a subset of crochet, was popular for creating canvases that were used for cross-stitch and other embellishing stitches.

Two women who advanced the craft are profiled in Richard Rutt's 1987 book, *History of Hand Knitting*. Contemporaries yet rivals, Cornelia Mee and Mlle Riego de la Branchardiere were both born in England in the early 1800s and both published numerous works on knitting, crochet, and lacework during their careers. Both made similar claims that they alone invented crochet.

Cornelia Mee published *Manual of Knitting, Netting and Crochet*, her first work, in 1842. Along with her sister, Mary Battle Austin, they started a monthly magazine, *The Worktable Magazine*, which acknowledged that the homemaker's highest bliss was to "minister to the wants, the convenience or the pleasure of those she loves." The crochet projects printed in their magazine provided for the "fabrication of those articles calculated to accomplish those desirable ends." Their patterns—or recipes, as they were called at the time—were known for being pretty but not frivolous. Mee is credited with dominating the polite English knitting and crochet circles for 30 years and was known as an innovator.

Mlle Riego de la Branchardiere published many crochet, knitting, lacework, and tatting patterns between 1846 and 1888 and, like Mee, claimed to be the inventor of crochet. However, she is credited with popularizing Irish crochet. In 1847 she published a knitting book that was quite different from other knitting books of that period. She included illustrated instructions for learning the fundamentals of knitting. Other authors assumed the technical aspects were widely understood and didn't include instructional information. In 1851 at the Great Exhibition held in London, she won the only gold medal awarded for crochet. She also claimed to be the first professional knitter for the royal family. Throughout her career she complained that her work was being pirated and plagiarized, and in all probability it was. Due to the high demand for designs, patterns were frequently reprinted with little regard for the designer or copyrights.

During this period, while well-bred English ladies were crocheting for the benefit of their loved ones, some other Europeans considered crochet a pointless luxury, perhaps due to its simplicity. For a time, Prussian schools forbade the teaching of crochet. However, many of the teachers ignored the ban and continued to teach the technique.

Interestingly, the early magazines didn't contain any advertisements. Paid advertising by yarn and thread manufacturers is a twentieth-century phenomenon. But soon after the beginning of advertising, manufacturers began publishing their own pattern books, a practice that continues today. This allows the yarn manufacturers more control of their industry and provides oversight to the craft. As a result, today's crochet is a mainstream craft that is considered to be on the forefront of fashion.

getting HOOKED

A very simple tool, fundamentally a stick or rod with a hook on one end, is all that is needed to crochet. For Tunisian crochet, only a longer rod is required. Crochet hooks can be made from plastic, wood, bamboo, or aluminum. All hooks have some basic features that aid in forming the stitches.

- **Tip, point, or head.** This end of the hook is used to catch and move the yarn. It needs to be small and pointy enough to slide through previous loops. Some tips are more pointed than others.
- **Throat.** This is the slender portion of the hook that widens into the full diameter of the shaft. The shape varies from a straight throat to a tapered throat into the hook. Personal preference will dictate the type of hook to use.
- **Shaft.** This section of the hook holds the stitches. The diameter of this portion creates the size of the stitch. The hook size refers to this portion of the hook. Choosing

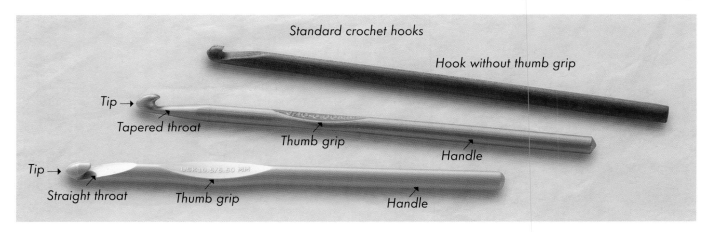

Standard crochet hooks

Hook without thumb grip

Tip →

Tapered throat

Thumb grip

Handle

Tip →

Straight throat

Thumb grip

Handle

the hook for the correct gauge is important for the outcome of the project. The size of hook stated in the pattern isn't necessarily the hook for you. Swatching with different sizes of hooks will determine which size of hook to use.

- **Thumb grip.** This flat section of the hook allows for a more comfortable grasp. A hook with a thumb grip is unworkable for Tunisian crochet, however, as the stitches will not slide over this flattened and flared area. A few manufacturers make crochet hooks without the thumb-grip area, and these hooks can be used for standard crochet, small Tunisian crochet projects, or those that have only a small number of stitches on the hook, such as entrelac.

- **Handle.** This is the remaining part of the hook and rests against the palm of your hand.

TUNISIAN CROCHET HOOK

Notice the similarities between the regular crochet hook and a Tunisian crochet hook. Both hooks have a tip and a throat. The Tunisian crochet hook is much longer, and there is no thumb grip. A button-type stopper

on the end keeps the stitches from sliding off the back end.

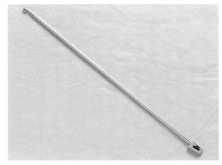

Tunisian crochet hook with long handle

Some Tunisian crochet hooks have a wire cable or extender to hold the stitches. This is particularly helpful when working a piece with a lot of stitches, such as an afghan. The length of the extension needs to be long enough to hold all the stitches. Generally, the length of the resulting piece can be up to three times the length of the extension.

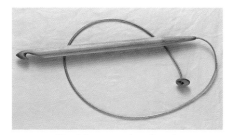

Tunisian crochet hook with cable and stopper

Sets of interchangeable crochet hook kits are now available and offer a range of hook sizes and cable lengths, making the kits particularly versatile.

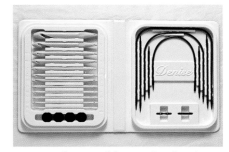

Interchangeable crochet hooks

The kits are capable of accommodating small as well as large projects. While the extension cord needs to be long enough to accommodate all the stitches, a cord that is too long tends to annoyingly flap and dangle when not holding stitches. To configure a hook for a specific project, select the hook size and desired cord length and snap together, place the stopper on the end, and you're ready to begin. If partway through the project, you add a considerable number of stitches or decide you would prefer to give the stitches more room, you can easily attach a longer cord. As the project progresses and fewer stitches need to be accommodated or you find the length of the cord irritating, select a shorter cord and attach it. The hooks, without the extension cord, can also be used for regular crochet, eliminating the need to purchase both regular crochet hooks and Tunisian crochet hooks.

Hooks come in different sizes and are labeled with either a number, letter, and/or metric measurement (see "Crochet Hook Sizes" on page 78). Relying on the metric measurement, the actual millimeter size of the hook, is the most reliable measure since, depending on the manufacturer and the country where the hook is manufactured, the number and/or letter may vary. Each pattern suggests the size of hook to use in number, letter, and metric size. But remember, you should work a gauge swatch and adjust the hook size if necessary. In general, the thicker the yarn, the larger the hook. A yarn label usually states a suggested hook size, but that relates to regular crochet. Because of the dense nature of Tunisian crochet stitches, a hook several sizes larger than what you would use for regular crochet is recommended.

GETTING A GRIP

Remember that you want to be in command of your work, so you need to have easy control over your hook and yarn. There are several ways of controlling both your hook and yarn. Experiment with the various suggestions and go with whichever technique seems most comfortable and gives the most consistent stitches.

Regular crochet invloves two common ways of holding the hook. For the "pencil" method, grasp the hook between your thumb and forefinger, just like you would a pencil, with the handle of the hook resting along the side of your hand near your knuckles. For the "knife" method, grasp the hook overhand, just as you would hold a knife.

Hold like a pencil

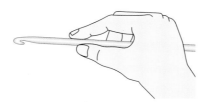

Hold like a knife

For Tunisian crochet, the "knife" method is more effective, because of the number of stitches that accumulate on the hook during the forward pass.

If you control your hook with your right hand, control the yarn with your left. Left-handed individuals may prefer to reverse this and hold the hook in their left hand and yarn in the right; by propping the book in front of a mirror and looking at the illustrations reflected in the mirror, you can easily learn. Or, since both hands are used, most left-handed individuals in my Tunisian crochet classes learn the same way as right-handed students.

The way you hold the yarn controls the tension. An even tension will give a uniform stitch and consistent gauge. With consistent and correct tension, the yarn will flow easily and smoothly through your fingers.

Several ways of managing the yarn can be used. Practice the various ways of holding the yarn, but don't worry if your preferred method is a little different from these methods.

- Wrap the working yarn around your index finger.
- Wrap the working yarn around your little finger, under the next two fingers, and over the top of your forefinger (pointer finger).
- Wrap the working yarn around your little finger, then over the top of your other fingers.
- Without wrapping the yarn around your little finger, close your fingers over the yarn.

❧ TUTORIAL ❧

Tunisian crochet produces a richly textured, wovenlike fabric. Each row consists of two passes: a forward pass, worked from right to left, where stitches accumulate on the hook; and the return pass, worked from left to right, where stitches are worked off the hook. The work is never turned unless the pattern gives explicit instructions to do so. For tidy beginning and ending edges, a regular crochet hook, usually one or two sizes smaller than the Tunisian crochet hook, is used for the foundation chain and bind off. The pattern instructions will suggest what size hook to use.

IT ALL BEGINS WITH A SLIPKNOT

A slipknot is an adjustable loop, like a noose, that is tightened on your crochet hook, anchoring the yarn to the hook.

About 6" from the end of the yarn, make a circle. Pull the strand of yarn attached to the ball forward

through the circle. Adjust this loop to fit snugly, but not too tightly, around the shaft of the hook.

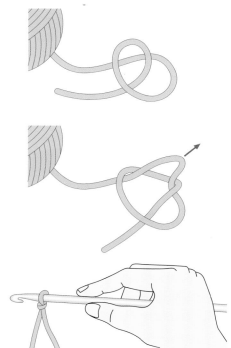

THEN COMES THE CHAIN STITCH

The chain stitch is the base or foundation upon which the remaining rows of stitches are built.

With the slipknot on the shaft of the hook, yarn over (YO) by wrapping

the working yarn around the hook from the back, over the hook, to the front and pulling through the slipknot—one loop on the hook. Adjust the size of the loop so that it approximates the size of the slipknot; it should be snug but not tight around the shaft of the hook. Repeat in this manner, pulling each new loop through the previously made loop until you have the desired number of chains. You will have to readjust your grasp on the yarn after several chains to keep even tension on the stitches.

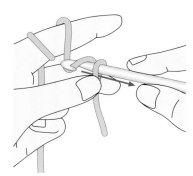

Anatomy of a Chain

Understanding the basic makeup of the chain will make it easier to count and lay down the basic foundation row for Tunisian crochet. Look closely at the chain and you will see V stitches on one side and, when the chain is turned over, the purl bump on the other side. The purl bump is sometimes referred to as the butt or camel's hump. The first row of stitches is worked either into the top loop of the V or into the back bump. Some sources suggest that working into the back bump lessens the amount of curl along the bottom edge; however, blocking and the final applied crochet edge will tame any curl that results. Unless a pattern specifically states where to insert the hook, use your favorite method—just be consistent within the pattern.

Foundation forward pass
through top loop of V

Foundation forward pass
through back bump

Counting Chains

To count chains, slightly stretch out the entire chain, removing any twists or kinks, with the V facing to the front. The loop on the hook is never counted, nor is the slipknot at the beginning of the chain.

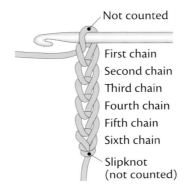

Not counted
First chain
Second chain
Third chain
Fourth chain
Fifth chain
Sixth chain
Slipknot
(not counted)

Front of chain

NOW YOU CREATE THE FOUNDATION

To create the foundation row for Tunisian crochet, make the initial chain using a regular crochet hook one or two sizes smaller than the Tunisian crochet hook you used to obtain the pattern's gauge. Using a hook that is too large will result in a loose and sloppy-looking cast-on edge. A chain is required for each stitch in the pattern. Once the chain is complete, replace the regular crochet hook with the Tunisian crochet hook in the size required to obtain gauge.

You're now ready to begin the foundation row. The foundation row is worked in two passes, a forward and a return pass. Both passes must be worked to complete the foundation row.

The forward pass is worked from right to left into the chain. The first chain from the hook is always skipped; this is the chain already attached to the loop on the hook. Insert the hook into the second chain, yarn over, and pull up a loop—two loops on the hook. Insert the hook into the next chain and pull up another loop—three loops on the hook. Continue across the row, adding another loop on the hook for each chain worked. Once the last chain is worked, there should be the same number of loops on the hook as there are chains. Never turn the work unless specifically told to do so. When counting stitches, count after completing the forward pass.

The return pass is worked from left to right as the stitches are worked off the hook. Make a yarn over and pull through one loop on the hook. The beginning of the return pass is always worked through one loop unless otherwise indicated. Then make another yarn over and pull through two loops on the hook. Repeat the yarn over and pull through two loops across the row until one loop remains on the hook.

The foundation row is now complete and the one loop remaining on the hook is the start of the next row.

Anatomy of Tunisian Crochet

A close look at the anatomy or structure of the stitches will identify the four fundamental strands that make up the fabric created with Tunisian crochet. As with knitting and crochet, where the hook is inserted will in part define the stitch.

The vertical bar is created during the forward pass and has a front and back bar. The horizontal bar is

created during the return pass and has an upper and a lower strand.

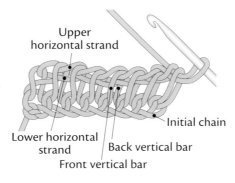

Upper horizontal strand

Lower horizontal strand

Back vertical bar

Front vertical bar

Initial chain

THEN YOU WORK THE TUNISIAN SIMPLE STITCH (Tss)

This is the basic stitch and, like all Tunisian stitches, is worked in two passes, the forward pass and the return pass. Both passes must be worked to complete a row.

On the forward pass, the first stitch or loop (which was created by the last stitch of the return pass from the previous row and is now attached to the loop on the hook) is always skipped. Insert the hook from right to left behind the front of the next vertical bar between the front and back bars. Yarn over and pull up a loop, keeping it on the hook—two loops on the hook. Do this behind

each vertical bar across the row to the last vertical bar, accumulating loops on the hook as you work to the last stitch.

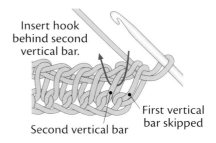

Insert hook behind second vertical bar.

Second vertical bar

First vertical bar skipped

The last stitch in the forward pass needs a little extra attention to keep the left edge smooth and neat. Insert the hook behind the last vertical bar and the strand that lies directly behind it. To properly identify this strand, look closely, follow this strand upward, and notice that it becomes the lower horizontal strand. With the hook inserted under both of these strands, yarn over and pull up the last loop.

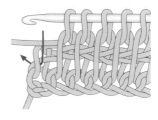

The return pass is made exactly the same way as the return pass of the foundation return pass (see page 13). Working from left to right, yarn over and pull through one loop on the hook, *yarn over and pull through two loops on the hook. Repeat from * until one loop remains. This last loop is the first stitch of the next forward row.

Continue working forward and return passes for the desired length of the piece. Count loops at the end of the forward pass to be sure you maintain the correct number of stitches. Look at the side edges to be sure they are clean and neat. The troubleshooting chart at right along with a little practice will help correct any common problems you may experience.

TROUBLESHOOTING FOR COMMON PROBLEMS	
Problem	Correction
Left-hand edge loose and uneven	Insert the hook through both the last vertical bar and the strand directly behind it. Keep tension snug and firm without pulling too tight.
Right-hand edge loose and uneven	When working the first stitch, keep tension snug but not too tight.
Work slants to the right	Work the first stitch into the front of the second vertical bar instead of the first vertical bar.
Losing stitches	Work the last vertical bar. Do not work two vertical bars together.
Gaining stitches	Work across the row through the front vertical bars, not the horizontal bars or spaces.

FINALLY, YOU BIND OFF

The most common way to end your work is to bind off using a slip stitch. Other stitch patterns may require a different bind off and will be stated with each pattern.

At the beginning of the forward pass, insert the hook behind the next vertical bar, yarn over and pull through the vertical bar and the loop on the hook—one loop remains on the hook. Repeat, working from right to left across the row. Fasten off the last loop. To prevent the bind-off row from being too loose, change to a smaller crochet hook as directed in the pattern.

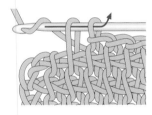

You now have the essential information needed to cast on, to work in Tunisian simple stitch, and to bind off. With a few practice swatches, your stitches will become smooth and even.

ADDITIONAL STITCHES

In addition to the Tunisian simple stitch (Tss) that you already learned, there are two other basic stitches: the Tunisian knit stitch (Tks) and the Tunisian purl stitch (Tps).

Tunisian Knit Stitch (Tks)

The Tunisian knit stitch creates a stitch that looks very similar to the knit stitch and serves as the basis for other fancy stitches. The resulting fabric is even denser than the Tunisian simple stitch. The patterns will specify what size hook to use to achieve a more supple fabric.

For the forward pass, working from right to left and with the yarn in back, insert the hook from front to back between the vertical bars and under the horizontal strands, yarn over and pull up a loop. Repeat across the row. Work the return pass as for the Tunisian simple stitch (page 15).

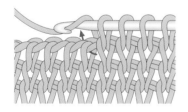

Tunisian Purl Stitch (Tps)

At first, the Tunisian purl stitch seems awkward and difficult to work, but with a little practice, it becomes more manageable and comfortable.

These stitches are made with the yarn held to the front of the work. Working from right to left and with the yarn in front, insert the hook as if to work the Tunisian simple stitch (behind the front vertical bar and between the front and back bars), yarn over and pull up a loop. Repeat across the row. Work the return pass as for the Tunisian simple stitch (page 15).

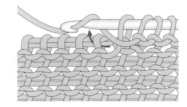

Yarn Over (YO)

A yarn over will make a hole in the fabric and is used to work lace stitches. Used on its own, it creates an additional stitch. The pattern will give directions on how to maintain the correct number of stitches by either pairing the increase of the yarn over with a skipped stitch or decreasing a stitch.

To work, wrap the yarn over the hook and, without pulling through a loop, continue as directed in the pattern.

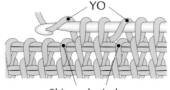

YO

Skipped stitches

SHAPING TECHNIQUES: INCREASES AND DECREASES

To create anything other than a square or rectangular piece of fabric, you need to incorporate increases and decreases into the work. You can make an increase and a decrease in single increments or in multiples. Make them within a row or at either of the side edges. You can make decreases by working multiple stitches together into one stitch, binding off, or leaving some stitches unworked.

Single Increase

A single increase, a Make 1 (M1), adds one loop between two stitches. On the forward pass, insert the hook into the space between the loop on the hook and the next vertical bar, yarn over and pull up a loop—one increase made. Continue by working the next vertical bar as usual.

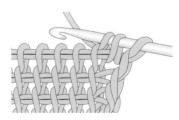

Right-Edge Multiple Increases

When multiple stitches need to be added at the same time, they are added at the end of the return pass, before beginning the forward pass, by simply chaining the required number of stitches. Begin the next forward pass by working the foundation forward pass into each chain, then continue working a forward pass for your pattern in the usual manner.

Chain

Left-Edge Multiple Increases

Multiple increases can be made at the left edge by working across to the end of the row where the additional stitches are required. Remove the hook and set the piece aside. With a separate piece of the same yarn, chain the required number of increases and remove the hook. Return to the first piece, put it back on the hook, and then work the foundation forward pass into each chain. Work the foundation

return pass across the newly added stitches, then continue with the return pass across to the end of the row.

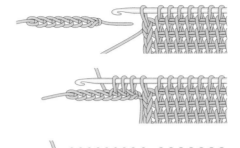

Tunisian Simple Stitch Two Together (Tss2tog) Decrease

Working from right to left on a forward pass, insert the hook under the front vertical bars of two stitches together, yarn over and pull through both vertical bars—one decrease made.

Tunisian Simple Stitch Three Together (Tss3tog) Decrease

Working from right to left on a forward pass, insert the hook under the front vertical bars of three stitches together, yarn over and pull through all three stitches—two decreases made.

Right-Edge Multiple Decreases

Working from right to left, use the slip-stitch bind off (see page 15) for the desired number of stitches you want to decrease.

Slipped stitches

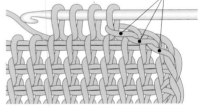

Left-Edge Multiple Decreases

Working from right to left, leave the required number of stitches you want to decrease unworked. This may give the impression that an unfinished edge will result, but generally, this edge is later worked into a seam, or a crochet edge is applied.

Stitches unworked

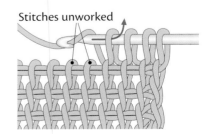

CHANGING COLOR

Color changes can be done at either the left- or right-hand edge or, for that matter, anywhere within the row. The pattern will specify where the color change is to occur.

A color change at the right-hand edge is made at the end of the return pass when two loops remain on the hook. Move the color to be dropped to the right, bring the new color to the left and up over the hook, and pull up a loop through both loops on the hook. This locks the new color on top of the color

being dropped, keeping the strand close to the edge. The forward pass is then made in the new color.

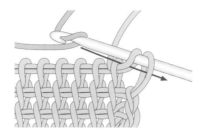

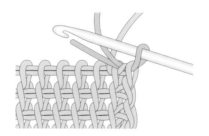

A color change at the left-hand edge is made after the forward pass is completed. Begin with the first stitch of the return pass. Move the color you are dropping to the left and drop it, bring the new color up and over the old yarn, yarn over and pull through one loop, yarn over and pull through two loops; continue with the return pass as usual.

When working a stripe pattern, do not cut the yarn when the color is changed. Rather, carry the yarn up the side.

⤫ ready, set, but BEFORE YOU BEGIN ⤬

While you may be less familiar with some of the techniques used in Tunisian crochet, your knowledge of crochet and knitting will serve you well. The principles of working with yarn—whether knitting, crocheting, or working Tunisian crochet—are the same.

The Craft Yarn Council of America developed guidelines for determining skill levels; see page 78. (All these projects fall within the first three categories: beginner, easy, and intermediate.) Once you know the basics, a little practice in the specific

stitch pattern should be enough to build your skill level so that you can successfully complete any of the projects.

Start by visiting your local yarn store. If you want your completed project to look like the one in the book, choose the specific yarn or one with similar gauge, fiber, and structure. If you choose a yarn that is markedly different, understand that the end product will be markedly different—although it may still result in a very attractive and striking garment. The choice is yours.

The unknown of selecting and substituting yarn can be reduced by reading the yarn label. The label will state the hook size and gauge, yardage, fiber content, and care instructions. When substituting yarn, you want to pick a yarn that is a similar thickness. To make this selection easier, there are universal symbols indicating yarn weights (thickness); see page 77. The weight of the yarn used for each project is indicated with a corresponding symbol. Comparing the yarn-weight symbol to the standard yarn-weight chart will identify the type of yarn you should be looking for. Keep in mind that Tunisian crochet naturally creates a dense, thick fabric, and the projects are worked on larger hook sizes than would normally be used for either regular crochet or knitting.

Be sure to purchase a sufficient amount of yarn. The directions, under the heading of "Materials," give the number of skeins for each project and the yardage for each skein. Multiply the number of balls times the amount of yarn on each ball to determine the total number of yards required for the specific project. Once you have found a yarn that you would like to use, read the label to determine the yardage for that skein. Divide the total number of yards required for your project by the amount in each ball of the substituted yarn to determine the number of balls you should purchase. Sometimes you will have some yarn left over; this is a lot better than running short. If you have ever run short and were unable to purchase enough yarn to complete a project, you understand the importance of purchasing enough. Also, if you want to alter a project, make it larger or longer, remember to purchase more yarn. Use the chart on page 78 to help you convert metric measurements.

GENEROUS GAUGE

Be generous with your gauge swatches; consider them an investment toward a successful project. The suggested gauge given for each Tunisian crochet project will not correspond to the gauge suggested on the yarn label. Tunisian crochet produces a dense, thick fabric, so a larger hook size is used to create a lighter fabric. The stitch pattern greatly affects the number of stitches per inch. The only way to know if you have the right combination of yarn and hook is to make a gauge swatch. In some cases, you'll need to make another and another.

The gauge swatch is the perfect way to master your technique and the specific stitch pattern. It should be at least 4" square; larger is even better. The gauge given as part of the instructions will indicate the number of stitches for 4", but check the pattern-stitch-multiple number. For example, if the multiple is 9 stitches plus 4 stitches, you will need 22 chains (9 stitches x 2 repeats + 4 stitches = 22 stitches). This will allow you to work two complete pattern repeats. Work in the pattern until the piece measures 4", or longer if there are more rows to the pattern repeat. Measure the width of the swatch and divide by 22 stitches for the number of stitches per inch. If the number of stitches per inch is less than the desired number, go down a hook size and repeat the pattern. If the number of stitches per inch is more than the desired number, go up a hook size.

All gauges for the projects are given after blocking, using the stated blocking method. Stitch patterns before blocking are dense, often bunch together, and hide the beauty of the pattern. Blocking will open up, spread, and even out the stitches; it will also give the proper dimensions to the finished piece. Amazingly, a blocked piece looks different from the unblocked piece. Several different methods for blocking are discussed on page 77, and each project specifies a suggested blocking method.

You may have to repeat the swatching process several times to get to the stated stitch gauge. This is not a waste of time. If you want the project to turn out as described, you need to achieve the proper gauge. Feel free to try something different; you may end up with a greatly enhanced and desirable piece of work. However, if you want to create a piece that looks like the photo, work up a swatch with the correct gauge before beginning.

The good news with gauge is that, generally, you don't have to deal with row gauge. Most of the patterns are written in inches, rather than rows per inch. Row gauge is only specified in the patterns where it is important.

Before going on to the actual project, you may want to work a few more pattern repeats to become more familiar with the techniques used in the pattern stitch. Remember: it's an investment in the success of the project.

REVERSIBLE kickshaw

Skill Level: Easy ●■□□

Finished Measurements

Place Mat: Approx 20" x 14"

Coaster: Approx 4" x 4"

MATERIALS

Fantasy Naturale from Plymouth Yarns (100% mercerized cotton; 100 g; 140 yds)

A 3 skeins in color 9705

B 2 skeins in color 8011

Size H-8 (5 mm) Tunisian crochet hook or size required to obtain gauge

Size G-6 (4.5 mm) crochet hook or two sizes smaller than Tunisian crochet hook

Gauge: 15 sts = 4" in Tss

Notes

Color change is done at left edge with first stitch of return pass (see page 18).

Consider working coasters as a gauge swatch.

The solid-color coaster is a perfect beginner project.

STITCH GUIDE

Foundation forward pass: *Insert hook in next ch, YO and pull up lp, leave lp on hook; rep from * across ch. Do NOT turn work.

Foundation return pass: YO and pull through 1 lp, *YO and pull through 2 lps; rep from * until 1 lp rem on hook.

Tss forward pass: *Insert hook from right to left behind front vertical bar, YO and pull up lp, leave lp on hook; rep from * across row.

Tss return pass with yarn change: With new yarn, YO and pull through 1 lp, *YO and pull through 2 lps; rep from * across row until 1 lp rem on hook.

Sl st BO: *Insert hook from right to left behind front vertical bar, YO and pull through 2 lps; rep from * until sts are bound off.

PLACE MAT (MAKE 2)

With A and smaller hook, ch 74.

Switch to Tunisian hook. Work foundation forward pass—74 lps on hook. Work foundation return pass.

Work in Tss until piece measures 2". Cont in Tss, changing to B before return pass.

Cont in established patt, changing color at every left edge until piece measures 13½", ending with return pass and yarn A.

With smaller hook, sl st BO. Do not fasten off.

Cont with A and smaller crochet hook, sc around all sides, working 3 sc in each corner st. Fasten off and join with duplicate st (see page 75). Block using wet blocking method (see page 77) to smooth and even sts.

When it comes to serving kickshaws—those tasty morsels, treats, and delicacies—use these reversible place mats and coordinating coasters to create a perfectly laid-back, yet chic, ambiance. With one side splendidly striped and the other side sporting a more complex, tweedy surface, it's hard to agree on a favorite.

SOLID COASTER (MAKE 2)

With B and smaller hook, ch 15.

Switch to Tunisian crochet hook. Work foundation forward pass—15 lps on hook. Work foundation return pass.

Work in Tss until piece measures 4", ending with return pass.

With smaller crochet hook, sl st BO. Fasten off.

With A and smaller hook, sc around all sides, working 3 sc into each corner. Fasten off and join with duplicate st.

STRIPED COASTER (MAKE 2)

With A and smaller hook, ch 15.

Switch to Tunisian hook. Work foundation forward pass—15 lps on hook. Change to B and work foundation return pass.

Cont in Tss, changing color at every left edge until piece measures 4", ending with return pass and yarn A. Do not fasten off.

With smaller hook, sl st BO.

Cont with A and smaller hook, sc around all sides, working 3 sc into each corner. Fasten off and join with duplicate st.

SOFT SPOTS
gourmet popcorn

Soft spots help ease some
of the harshness of reality;
everyone needs a few.
In addition to providing
comfort, pillows can
quickly freshen up the
decor of any room.
As a stylish complement,
add one on the futon,
the couch, the bed, the
recliner, the patio glider,
or anywhere else you
seek comfort.

Pillow back

STITCH GUIDE

Foundation forward pass: *Insert hook in next ch, YO and pull up lp, leave lp on hook; rep from * across ch. Do NOT turn work.

Foundation return pass: YO and pull through 1 lp, *YO and pull through 2 lps; rep from * until 1 lp rem.

Tss forward pass: *Insert hook from right to left behind front vertical bar, YO and pull up lp, leave lp on hook; rep from * across row.

Tss return pass: YO and pull through 1 lp, *YO and pull through 2 lps; rep from * across row until 1 lp rem.

Sl st BO: *Insert hook from right to left behind front vertical bar, YO and pull through 2 lps; rep from * until sts are bound off.

POPCORN PATTERN

Popcorn: With A, work to position of popcorn, drop A, and ch 4 with B, drop B, and work Tss in next st with A, move ch 4 to front of work.

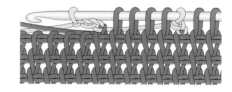

Skill Level: Beginner ■□□□

Finished Measurements: Approx 14" x 14"

MATERIALS

Summer Tweed from Rowan Yarns (70% silk, 30% cotton; 50 g; 108 m/118 yds) (4)

A 2 skeins in color 546 Loganberry

B 1 skein in color 529 Denim

Gossamer from Great Adirondack Yarn Co. (54% wool, 43% nylon, 3% polymide; 120 yds) (5)

C 1 skein in color 916 Pheasant

Size J-10 (6 mm) Tunisian crochet hook or size required to obtain gauge

Size I-9 (5.5 mm) or one size smaller than Tunisian crochet hook

14" x 14" pillow form

Gauge: 13 sts = 4" in Tss

Row 1: With A, work 4 sts (5 lps on hook), *make popcorn, work 4 sts with A; rep from * to end of row.

Rows 2–4: With A, work Tss forward and return passes.

Row 5: With A, work 7 sts (8 lps on hook), *make popcorn, work 4 sts with A; rep from * to last 3 sts, end Tss 3.

Rows 6–8: With A, work Tss forward and return passes.

Rep rows 1–8 for patt.

POPCORN SIDE

Color change is worked at right side, at end of return pass, when 2 loops rem on hook.

Popcorns are worked with yarn that is carried loosely on back side.

With A and smaller hook, ch 45.

Switch to Tunisian hook. Work foundation forward pass—45 lps on hook. Work foundation return pass.

Cont with A, work 5 rows of Tss forward and return passes.

Work popcorn patt 2 times (16 rows total), ending with return pass.

Work stripe pattern as follows: work 2 rows with B; work 1 row with A; repeat until piece measures 12½".

With A, work Tss until piece measures 13¾".

With smaller hook, sl st BO. Do not fasten off. Work sc along all edges, working 2 sc into each corner st. Fasten off and join with duplicate st.

TWEEDY-STRIPE SIDE

Color change is worked on left side at beg of return pass.

With A and smaller hook, ch 45.

Switch to Tunisian hook. Work foundation forward pass—45 lps on hook. Work foundation return pass.

Cont with A, work Tss forward and return passes until piece measures 3", ending with forward pass. Change to color B and work return pass. Cont in Tss, changing color at left edge until piece measures 12½". Cont in patt with A until piece measures 13¾".

With smaller hook, sl st BO. Do not fasten off. Work sc along all edges, working 2 sc into each corner st. Fasten off and join with duplicate st (see page 75).

FINISHING

Weave in ends. Block using pin-and-mist method (see page 77) to smooth and even sts.

Create seam on outside of work by placing WS tog and RS facing out. Using C and smaller hook, sc both sides tog, working 3 sc into each corner st and inserting pillow form before last side is completely closed. Join with sl st and change to larger hook. Ch 2, work 1 rnd of hdc all around, working 3 hdc into each corner st. Fasten off and join with duplicate st.

Popcorn and striped detail

~ ginger ROLL ~

Skill Level: Easy ■■□□

Finished Measurements: 5" x 14"

MATERIALS

5 skeins of Bonsai from Berroco (97% bamboo, 3% nylon; 1.75 oz/50 g; 77 yds/71 m) in color 4129 Pickled Ginger (4)

Size I-9 (5.5 mm) Tunisian crochet hook or size required to obtain gauge

Size H-8 (5 mm) crochet hook or one size smaller than Tunisian crochet hook

Size G-6 (4.5 mm) crochet hook for cord

5" x 14" neck-roll pillow form

Locking marker or safety pin

Gauge: 16 sts = 4" in patt

STITCH GUIDE

Foundation forward pass: *Insert hook in next ch, YO and pull up lp, leave lp on hook; rep from * across ch. Do NOT turn work.

Foundation return pass: YO and pull through 1 lp, *YO and pull through 2 lps; rep from * until 1 lp rem on hook.

Tss forward pass: *Insert hook from right to left behind front vertical bar, YO and pull up lp, leave lp on hook; rep from * across row.

Tss return pass: YO and pull through 1 lp, *YO and pull through 2 lps; rep from * across row until 1 lp rem.

Tps forward pass: *With yarn in front, insert hook from right to left behind front vertical bar, YO and pull up lp; rep from * across row.

Tps return pass: Work as for Tss return pass.

Tss2tog: Insert hook from right to left behind next 2 vertical bars, YO and pull through 2 bars, leave lp on hook.

Tss3tog: Insert hook from right to left behind next 3 vertical bars, YO and pull through 3 bars, leave lp on hook.

M1: Insert hook into sp between lp on hook and next vertical bar, YO and pull up lp.

Sl st BO: *Insert hook from right to left behind front vertical bar, YO and pull through 2 lps; rep from * until sts are bound off.

PATTERN STITCH

(Any number of sts)

Row 1: Work Tss forward and return passes.

Row 2: Work Tps forward pass to last st, Tss. Work return pass.

Rep rows 1 and 2 for patt.

FOUNDATION

With smaller hook, ch 76.

Switch to Tunisian hook. Work foundation forward pass—76 lps on hook. Work foundation return pass.

FIRST END

Row 1: Work Tss forward and return passes.

Row 2: Work Tps forward and return passes.

Row 3: Work Tss forward and return passes.

Row 4: Dec 37 sts as follows: *Tss2tog; rep from * across row to last st, Tss—39 sts. Work return pass.

Row 5: Dec 19 sts as follows: Tss3tog, *Tss2tog; rep from * across row—20 lps on hook. Work return pass.

Row 6: Work eyelet row as follows: *Tss2tog, YO; rep from * to last st, Tss. Work return pass.

Row 7: *Work Tss forward and return passes.

Row 8: Inc 16 sts as follows: Tss, *M1, Tss; rep from * across row—36 lps on hook. Work return pass.

Row 9: Inc 16 sts as follows: *Tss 2, M1; rep from * to last 3 sts, Tss 3—52 lps on hook. Work return pass.

Row 10: Work Tss forward and return passes.

Row 11: Inc 24 sts as follows: Tss, *Tss 2, M1; rep from * to last 3 sts, Tss 3—76 lps on hook. Work return pass. Mark this row with a locking marker or safety pin.

BODY OF PILLOW

Work in patt until piece measures 15" from marker, ending with row 1 return pass.

SECOND END

Row 1: Dec 25 sts as follows: *Tss2tog, Tss; rep from * to last st, Tss—51 lps on hook. Work return pass.

Row 2: Work Tss forward and return passes.

Row 3: Dec 15 sts as follows: Tss 2, *Tss2tog, Tss; rep from * to last 3 sts, Tss 3—36 lps on hook. Work return pass.

Row 4: Dec 16 sts as follows: Tss, *Tss2tog; rep from * to last 2 sts, Tss 2—20 lps on hook. Work return pass.

Row 5: Work eyelet row as follows: *Tss2tog, YO; rep to last 2 sts, Tss 2—20 lps on hook. Work return pass.

Row 6: Work Tss forward and return passes.

Row 7: Inc 19 sts as follows: *Tss, M1, YO and pull through lp; rep from * to last bar, end Tss—39 lps on hook. Work return pass.

Row 8: Inc 37 sts as follows: *M1, Tss; rep from * to last bar, Tss—76 lps on hook. Work return pass.

Row 9: Work Tss forward and return passes.

Row 10: Work Tps forward and return passes.

Row 11: Work Tss forward and return passes.

With smaller hook, sl st BO.

FINISHING

Weave in ends. Block using mist method (see page 77) to smooth and even sts.

Seam long edges together, inserting pillow form before completing seam.

Ties: With smaller hook, ch 50, turn, and work sc into each ch. Fasten off. Rep for second tie. Weave tie through eyelets. Tie snugly.

Pillow end

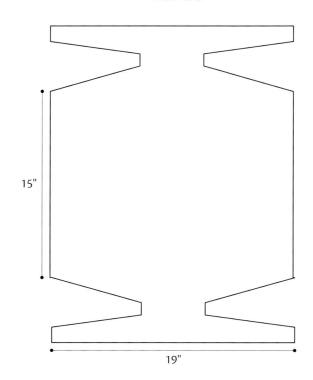

15"

19"

BUTTON down

Skill Level: Easy ◼◼◻◻

Finished Measurements: Approx 12½" x 15"

MATERIALS

4 skeins of Wool Classica from Manos del Uruguay (handspun pure wool; 3.5 oz/100 g; 138 yds/126 m) in color 30 (④)

Size I-9 (5.5 mm) Tunisian crochet hook or size required to obtain gauge

Size H-8 (5 mm) or one size smaller than Tunisian crochet hook

12" x 16" pillow form

3 large decorative buttons, 1¼" diameter

Gauge: 11 sts = 4" in patt

STITCH GUIDE

Foundation forward pass: *Insert hook in next ch, YO and pull up lp, leave lp on hook; rep from * across ch. Do NOT turn work.

Foundation return pass: YO and pull through 1 lp, *YO and pull through 2 lps; rep from * until 1 lp rem.

Tss forward pass: *Insert hook from right to left behind front vertical bar, YO and pull up lp, leave lp on hook; rep from * across row.

Tss return pass: YO and pull through 1 lp, *YO and pull through 2 lps; rep from * across row until 1 lp rem.

Tks forward pass: *Insert hook from front to back in the center of the next st and pull up lp, leave lp on hook; rep from * across row.

Tks return pass: Work as for Tss return pass.

Sl st BO: *Insert hook from right to left behind front vertical bar, YO and pull through 2 lps; rep from * until sts are bound off.

DIAGONAL STRIPE PATTERN (WORKED OVER 35 STS)

Row 1: (Tss 5, Tks 6) 3 times, Tss. Work return pass.

Row 2: Tss 4, (Tks 6, Tss 5) twice, Tks 6, Tss 2. Work return pass.

Row 3: Tss 3, (Tks 6, Tss 5) twice, Tks 6, Tss 3. Work return pass.

Row 4: Tss 2, (Tks 6, Tss 5) twice, Tks 6, Tss 4. Work return pass.

Row 5: Tss, (Tks 6, Tss 5) twice, Tks 6, Tss 5. Work return pass.

Row 6: (Tks 6, Tss 5) 3 times, Tss. Work return pass.

Row 7: Tks 5, (Tss 5, Tks 6) twice, Tss 5, Tks, Tss. Work return pass.

Row 8: Tks 4, (Tss 5, Tks 6) twice, Tss 5, Tks 2, Tss. Work return pass.

Row 9: Tks 3, (Tss 5, Tks 6) twice, Tss 5, Tks 3, Tss. Work return pass.

Row 10: Tks 2 (Tss 5, Tks 6) twice, Tss 5, Tks 4, Tss. Work return pass.

Row 11: Tks (Tss 5, Tks 6) twice, Tss 5, Tks 5, Tss. Work return pass.

Rep rows 1–11 for patt.

PILLOW

With smaller hook, ch 35. Switch to Tunisian hook. Work foundation forward pass—35 lps on hook. Work foundation return pass.

Work 6 rows of Tss forward and return passes.

Beg diagonal stripe patt and cont until piece measures 33".

Work 3 rows of Tss forward and return passes.

With smaller hook, sl st BO. Do not fasten off.

FINISHING

Cont with smaller hook, turn work and sc across BO edge, turn.

Buttonholes: Work along bound-off edge as follows:

> **Row 1:** With smaller hook, ch 1, sc across row, turn.
>
> **Row 2 (RS):** Ch 1, sc 6, (ch 3, sk next 3 sts, sc 7) twice, ch 3, sk next 3 sts, sc 6, turn.
>
> **Rows 3 and 4:** Ch 1, sc across. Fasten off.

Join yarn and work 2 rows of sc along CO edge.

Fold piece with RS tog, bringing CO edge 4" below finished buttonhole edge. Whipstitch (page 75) side seams tog. Turn pillow RS out. Position buttons opposite buttonholes and sew in place. Weave in ends. Block using mist method (see page 77) to smooth and even sts. Insert pillow form and button down.

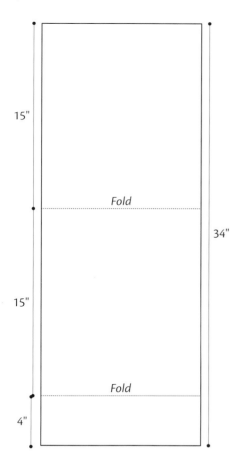

15"

Fold

34"

15"

Fold

4"

Pillow back

⊱ go GREEN ⊰

Skill Level: Easy ■■□□

Finished Measurements:
13" wide x 17½" long, excluding handles

MATERIALS

5 skeins of Grass from Plymouth Yarn (65% cotton, 35% hemp; 50 g; 115 yds) in color 9063 (4)

Size J-10 (6 mm) Tunisian crochet hook or size required to obtain gauge

Size I-9 (5.5 mm) crochet hook or one size smaller than Tunisian crochet hook

Gauge: 16 sts = 4" in Tss

STITCH GUIDE

Foundation forward pass: *Insert hook in next ch, YO and pull up lp, leave lp on hook; rep from * across ch. Do NOT turn work.

Foundation return pass: YO and pull through 1 lp, *YO and pull through 2 lps; rep from * until 1 lp rem.

Tss forward pass: *Insert hook from right to left behind front vertical bar, YO and pull up lp, leave lp on hook; rep from * across row.

Tss return pass: YO and pull through 1 lp, *YO and pull through 2 lps; rep from * across row until 1 lp rem.

Tks forward row: *Insert hook from front to back in center of next st, pull up lp, leave lp on hook; rep from * across row.

Tps forward row: *With yarn in front, insert hook from right to left under next vertical st, pull up lp, leave lp on hook; rep from * across row.

Tks and Tps return pass: Work as for Tss return pass.

Sl st BO: *Insert hook from right to left behind front vertical bar, YO and pull through 2 lps; rep from * until sts are bound off.

BASKET WEAVE PATTERN
(Multiple of 5 + 2)

Rows 1–4: *Tks 5 (6 lps on hook), Tps 5; rep from * to last st, Tss. Work return pass.

Rows 5–8: *Tps 5 (6 lps on hook), Tks 5; rep from * to last st, Tss. Work return pass.

Work rows 1–8 for patt.

TOTE

Bag is worked in one piece, beg at top open edge.

With smaller hook, ch 52.

Switch to Tunisian hook. Work foundation forward pass—52 lps on hook. Work foundation return pass.

Work 5 rows of Tss forward and return passes.

Work 10 rows of Basket Weave patt.

Work 10 rows of Tss forward and return passes.

Work 10 rows of Basket Weave patt.

Work 10 rows of Tss forward and return passes.

Work 10 rows of Basket Weave patt.

Work 10 rows of Tks forward and return passes (the 5th of these 10 rows is halfway point of bag).

Going green is easy with this durable tote, sturdy enough for library books, deep enough for baguettes, and sufficiently dense to keep keys and cell phone securely inside. The handles are long and thick enough to be worn comfortably over the shoulder. This tote works up quickly and makes a superb gift for family and friends.

Work 10 rows of Basket Weave patt.

Work 10 rows of Tss forward and return passes.

Work 10 rows of Basket Weave patt.

Work 10 rows of Tss forward and return passes.

Work 10 rows of Basket Weave patt.

Work 5 rows of Tss forward and return passes.

With smaller hook, work sl st BO.

HANDLES (MAKE 2)

With smaller hook, ch 90 sts. Switch to Tunisian hook. Work foundation forward pass—90 lps on hook. Work foundation return pass.

Work 5 rows of Tks forward and return passes.

With smaller hook, work sl st BO. With RS tog, allow CO and BO edges of handles to curl, and whipstitch long edges tog, leaving 1½" open at each end.

FINISHING

Fold bag in half with RS tog so that CO and BO edges are aligned. Whipstitch side seams tog. Turn bag RS out.

Attach handles: Position 1 handle on WS of bag; pin flat, with open end of handle 1½" from top of bag and 2" from side edge. Being careful not to twist handle, pin other end of handle 1½" from top and 2" from other side. Whipstitch securely in place. Rep for second handle.

Weave in all ends. Block pieces using wet blocking method (see page 77).

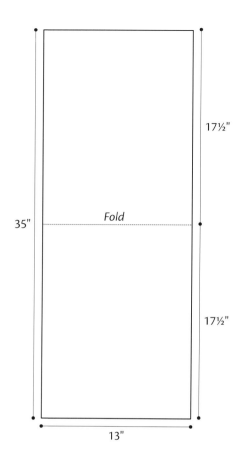

Flat end of handle sewn to inside of bag

rogue RIBS

Skill Level: Easy ◼◼◻◻

Finished Measurements: 7½" x 74"

MATERIALS

4 skeins of Linus from Knit One Crochet Too (47% wool, 30% acrylic, 23% alpaca; 50 g; 98 yds) in color 445 Copper Beech (4)

Size J-10 (6 mm) Tunisian crochet hook or size required for gauge

Size I-9 (5.5 mm) crochet hook or one size smaller than Tunisian crochet hook

Gauge: 13 sts = 4" in Tss

STITCH GUIDE

Foundation forward pass: *Insert hook in next ch, YO and pull up lp, leave lp on hook; rep from * across ch. Do NOT turn work.

Foundation return pass: YO and pull through 1 lp, *YO and pull through 2 lps; rep from * until 1 lp rem.

Tss forward pass: *Insert hook from right to left behind front vertical bar, YO and pull up lp, leave lp on hook; rep from * across row.

Tss return pass: YO and pull through 1 lp, *YO and pull through 2 lps; rep from * across row until 1 lp rem.

Tps forward pass: *With yarn in front, insert hook from right to left behind front vertical bar, YO and pull up lp; rep from * across row.

Tps return pass: Work as for Tss return pass.

Sl st Tss BO: *Insert hook from right to left behind front vertical bar, YO and pull through 2 lps on hook; rep from * for all Tss sts.

Sl st Tps BO: *With yarn in front, insert hook from right to left behind front vertical bar, YO and pull through 2 lps on hook; rep from * for all Tps sts.

RIBBING PATTERN

(Multiple of 7 + 4)

Forward pass: Tss into next 3 vertical bars (4 lps on hook), *Tps into next 3 vertical bars, Tss into next 4 vertical bars; rep from * across row.

Return pass: Work as for Tss return pass.

Work forward and return passes for patt.

SCARF

With smaller hook, ch 25.

Switch to Tunisian hook. Work foundation forward pass—25 lps on hook. Work foundation return pass.

Work in ribbing patt until piece measures 74", ending with return pass.

With smaller hook, work sl st BO in patt.

FINISHING

Weave in all ends. Block using mist method (see page 77) to smooth and even sts.

Easy ribbing with rogue bits of color add a touch of dynamism to this scarf. Long enough to be worn with finesse, warm enough to shield from the harsh elements, and soft enough to pamper. Reveal your mischievous side, yet maintain respectability with this classic ribbed scarf.

᭙ mystifying EMBRACE ᭙

Skill Level: Easy ◼◼☐☐

Finished Measurements: Approx 21" x 58", without crochet edge

MATERIALS

3 skeins of Smooshy from Dream in Color (100% superfine Australian merino superwash; 4 oz; 450 yds) in color VS140 Spring Tickle (**2**)

Size L-11 (8 mm) Tunisian crochet hook or size required to obtain gauge

Size K-10½ (6.5 mm) crochet hook or one size smaller than Tunisian crochet hook

Shawl pin (optional)

Gauge: 15 sts = 4" in patt

STITCH GUIDE

Foundation forward pass: *Insert hook in next ch, YO and pull up lp, leave lp on hook; rep from * across ch. Do NOT turn work.

Foundation return pass: YO and pull through 1 lp, *YO and pull through 2 lps; rep from * until 1 lp rem.

Tks forward pass: *Insert hook from front to back in the center of the next st, pull up lp, leave lp on hook; rep from * across row.

Tks return pass: YO and pull through 1 lp, *YO and pull through 2 lps; rep from * until 1 lp rem.

Sl st Tks BO: *Insert hook from front to back in center of next st, YO and pull through 2 lps on hook; rep from * until sts are bound off.

PATTERN

(Multiple of 3 + 2)

Every row: YO, Tks 3 (5 lps on hook), pass YO over 3 lps just made; *YO, Tks 3, pass YO over 3 lps; rep from * to last vertical bar, Tss. Work return pass as for Tss.

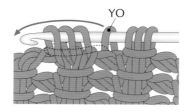

WRAP

Piece is worked as a rectangle, then twisted and seamed at short ends.

With smaller hook, ch 80.

Switch to Tunisian hook. Work foundation forward pass—80 lps on hook. Work foundation return pass.

Work in patt until piece measures 58" when slightly stretched.

With smaller hook, sl st Tks BO.

FINISHING

Block using wet blocking method (see page 77) before finishing.

To create Möbius strip, bring BO edge to CO edge and twist 180° before seaming, so that A meets A and B meets B (see diagram on page 40). With one WS to other RS, sl-st crochet (page 75) ends tog.

There is no mystery with this wrap, just a simple twist. You work it as a rectangle, then create a Möbius strip by rotating one end 180° before joining it to the other end. A single-sided edge runs along the entire wrap. Slip it over your head and experience a warm and gentle embrace.

With smaller hook, work edging all around as follows:

Rnd 1: Sc along continuous Möbius-strip edge, sl st to join.

Rnd 2: Ch 1, dc in sl st, *sk 1 st, sl st in next st, dc in same st; rep from * along continuous edge. Fasten off and join with duplicate st (see page 75).

Weave in ends. Mist seam.

Option

For a more classical wrap, leave as a rectangle. Sc around the entire edge, working 3 sc into each corner st.

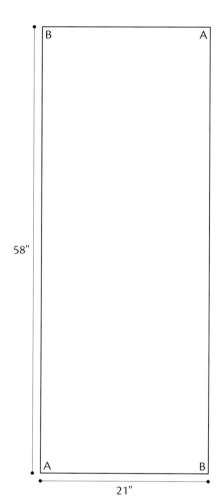

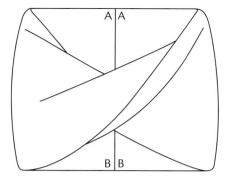

Pattern stitch close-up

❧ TRIPLE amusement ❧

Skill Level: Intermediate ■■■□

Finished Measurements: Approx 11½" wide x 10" deep, excluding handles

MATERIALS

Creative Focus Linen from Nashua Handknits (50% cotton, 50% linen; 3.5 oz/100 g; 220 yds/200 m) ❹

A 1 skein in color 1537 Salmon

B 1 skein in color 200 Natural

C 1 skein in color 1012 Espresso

Size H-8 (5 mm) Tunisian crochet hook or size required to obtain gauge

Size G-6 (4 mm) crochet hook or 2 sizes smaller than Tunisian crochet hook

D-shaped bamboo tote handles, 4¼" x 11½"

½ yd of 42"-wide cotton fabric for lining (optional)

Matching thread and sewing needle (optional)

Gauge: 18 sts = 4" in Tss

Notes

- Bag is worked in one piece, beginning with three separate handle tabs that are joined to form the body of the bag and ending with three separate tabs for the other handle.

- Right-edge color change is worked at end of return pass when 2 loops remain on hook.

- Left-edge color change is worked at beginning on return pass.

- Optional lining for bag can be hand or machine sewn.

STITCH GUIDE

Foundation forward pass: *Insert hook in next ch, YO and pull up lp, leave lp on hook; rep from * across ch. Do NOT turn work.

Foundation return pass: YO and pull through 1 lp, *YO and pull through 2 lps; rep from * until 1 lp rem.

Tss forward pass: *Insert hook from right to left behind front vertical bar, YO and pull up lp, leave lp on hook; rep from * across row.

Tss return pass: YO and draw through 1 lp, *YO and draw through 2 lps; rep from * across row until 1 lp rem.

Sl st BO: *Insert hook from right to left behind front vertical bar, YO and pull through 2 lps on hook; rep from * until sts are bound off.

WAFFLE PATTERN

Rows 1 and 3: With A, sk the first sp, *insert hook in sp between next vertical bars, YO and draw up lp, leave lp on hook; rep from * across to last vertical bar, Tss in last st. Work return pass.

Row 2: With B, *insert hook in sp between next vertical bars, YO and draw up lp, leave lp on hook; rep from * across to last 2 vertical bars, sk sp, and work Tss in last st. Work return pass.

Row 4: With C, *insert hook in sp between next vertical bars, YO and draw up lp, leave lp on hook; rep from * across to last 2 vertical bars, sk sp, and work Tss in last st. Work return pass.

Work rows 1–4 for patt.

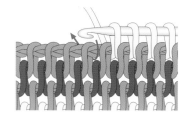

This handbag is simply indispensable; whether you're strolling along the waterfront, touring wine country, or hitting the urban streets, this is the perfect warm-weather bag. Enjoy the amusing color play with three colors worked over two different stitch patterns, resulting in a somewhat tribal look. With purchased bamboo handles and an option for lining the bag, it's ideal for holding your phone, sunglasses, and other basics.

BAG

Right tab: With A and smaller hook, ch 14.

Switch to Tunisian crochet hook. Work foundation forward pass—14 sts on hook. Work foundation return pass.

Work Tss until piece measures 3". Cut yarn, leaving 16" tail. Set piece aside.

Center tab: With A and smaller hook, ch 18.

Switch to Tunisian crochet hook. Work foundation forward pass—18 sts on hook. Work foundation return pass.

Work Tss until piece measures 3". Cut yarn, leaving 20" tail. Set piece aside.

Left tab: With A and smaller hook, ch 14.

Switch to Tunisian crochet hook. Work foundation forward pass—14 sts on hook. Work foundation return pass.

Work Tss until piece measures 3". Do not cut yarn. Set aside.

Setup pass: With right tab, use tail to work Tss forward pass, leave lps on hook. With center tab, use tail to work forward pass, leave lps on hook. With left tab, work forward pass.

Return joining pass: Work Tss return pass across left tab, ch 3, cont return pass across center tab, ch 3, cont return pass across right tab. Tabs are now joined.

Work Tss across right tab, work foundation forward pass across 3 chs, cont Tss across center tab, work foundation forward pass across 3 chs, Tss across right tab. Work return pass.

Work 3 rows of Tss forward and return passes.

Cont in Tss, working colors as follows:

Row 1: Right edge, change to B, work forward pass. Left edge, change to C, work return pass.

Row 2: Right edge, change to A, work forward and return passes.

Row 3: Right edge, change to C, work forward pass. Left edge, change to B, work return pass.

Row 4: Right edge, change to A, work forward and return passes.

Row 5: Right edge, change to B, work forward pass. Left edge, change to C, work return pass.

Row 6: Right edge, change to A, work forward pass. Left edge, change to B, work return pass.

Row 7: Right edge, change to C, work forward pass. Left edge, change to A, work return pass.

Row 8: Right edge, change to B, work forward and return passes.

Row 9: Right edge, change to A, work forward and return passes.

Row 10: Right edge, change to C, work forward pass. Left edge, change to A, work return pass.

With A, work 2 rows of Tss.

Beg waffle patt and cont until piece measures 10", ending with row 3.

With A, work 3 rows of Tss forward and return passes.

Cont in Tss, working colors as follows:

Row 1: Right edge, change to C, work forward pass. Left edge, change to A, work return pass.

Row 2: Cont with A, work forward pass. Left edge, change to B, work return pass.

Row 3: Cont with B, work forward pass. Left edge, change to C, work return pass.

Row 4: Cont with C, work forward pass. Left edge, change to A, work return pass.

Row 5: Cont with A, work forward pass. Left edge, change to B, work return pass.

Row 6: Cont with B, work forward pass. Left edge, change to C, work return pass.

Row 7: Right edge, change to A, work forward and return passes.

Row 8: Right edge, change to C, work forward pass. Left edge, change to B, work return pass.

Row 9: Right edge, change to A, work forward and return passes.

Row 10: Right edge, change to B, work forward pass. Left edge, change to C, work return pass.

Right edge, change to A, work 3 rows of Tss, work forward and return passes.

Right tab: Work first 14 sts, leaving rem sts unworked, until tab measures 3". Sl st BO. Cut yarn, leaving 12" tail.

Center tab: Attach yarn at base of tab just completed and sl st BO 3 sts. Tss next 18 sts, leaving rest of sts unworked, until tab measures 3". Sl st BO. Cut yarn, leaving 18" tail.

Left tab: Attach yarn at base of tab just completed and sl st BO 3 sts. Tss next 14 sts, leaving rest of sts unworked, until tab measures 3". Sl st BO. Cut yarn, leaving 18" tail.

FINISHING

With A and smaller hook, beg at first color change, sc along side to last color change. Fasten off and join using duplicate st (see page 75). Block piece using mist method (see page 77) to smooth and even sts. For optional lining see sidebar. Fold bag in half with RS tog and side edges aligned. Whipstitch (page 75) side seams tog from top of first color change to bottom fold.

Turn bag RS out. Fold tabs over bar of handle and sew each tab securely to third row of Tss above color change.

Optional Lining

Cut lining before seaming bag. Use piece as pattern and cut lining, adding ⅝" for seam allowance. With RS of lining fabric tog, using needle and thread or sewing machine, sew side and bottom seams. When bag is finished, place lining in bag. Fold top edge of fabric to inside along first color change and hand sew lining to bag.

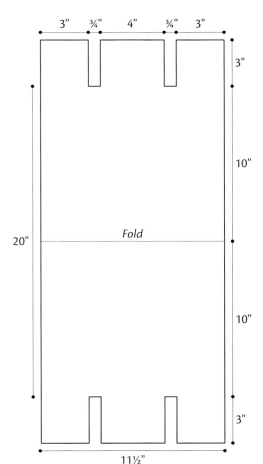

Bag with optional lining

MOTIVATED heretic

Skill Level: Intermediate ■■■□

Finished Measurements: Approx 16" x 85", without crochet edge

MATERIALS

9 skeins of Silk Garden from Noro (45% silk, 45% kid mohair, 10% lamb's wool; 50 g; 100 m) in color 87

Size K-10½ (6.5 mm) Tunisian crochet hook (or crochet hook without thumb grip) or size required to obtain gauge

Size N/P-15 (10 mm) crochet hook for crochet edge

Shawl pin (optional)

Gauge: 13 sts = 4" in Tss

STITCH GUIDE

Tss forward pass: *Insert hook from right to left behind front vertical bar, YO and pull up lp, leave lp on hook; rep from * across row.

Tss return pass: *YO and pull through 2 lps on hook; rep from * until 1 lp rem.

M1: Insert hook in sp between next 2 sts as directed, pull up lp.

Sc BO: *Insert hook from right to left behind front vertical bar, YO and pull up lp, YO and pull through 2 lps on hook; rep from * across until 1 lp rem.

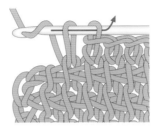

SHAWL

With larger hook, very loosely ch 31.

Change to smaller hook and work 5 base triangles (see sidebar on page 48).

Work tiers 2 and 3 until piece measures 80" or desired length, ending with tier 2. Turn work.

Work 5 end triangles. Do not cut yarn.

FINISHING

Cont with yarn from last triangle and smaller hook, sc around all edges, working 3 sc into each corner st. Sl st to join, ch 1. Work second round of sc, working 3 sc into each corner st. Fasten off and join with duplicate st (see page 75).

Weave in ends. Block using wet method (see page 77) to smooth and even sts. Adding a no-rinse wool wash to the water will help soften the fibers.

Notes

- Either a Tunisian crochet hook or standard crochet hook without thumb grip can be used because the maximum number of stitches on the hook is 8.

- While Tunisian crochet projects are usually worked without turning the work, this project is an exception. Turn the work at the end of each tier and continue as directed.

- The return pass in this project is worked differently than a standard return pass (see stitch guide at left).

- When picking up loops, insert the hook through both loops of the previous work.

- Work your gauge swatch using the Tunisian simple stitch (Tss).

- The initial chain is a multiple of 6 chains plus 1 chain. To alter size of the shawl, subtract or add multiples of 6 chains.

- The initial chain is made using a hook 3 sizes larger than the Tunisian crochet hook.

How many ends does a mild-mannered woman need to weave in before she turns into a heretic? Well, this totally reversible entrelac shawl will not push anyone to the limit, because a rule was broken. Instead of having to cut and tie on new yarn at the beginning and end of each tier of blocks, the work is turned, creating alternating tiers of right- and wrong-sided textured blocks. Take pleasure in becoming a nonconformist and know that there will only be a few ends to weave in.

ENTRELAC

Entrelac is a technique that uses interconnected squares and triangles to create a lovely textured diamond pattern. Working with variegated yarn and turning the work before beginning the next tier adds richness and interest.

When picking up stitches, inserting the hook into the correct space will produce perfectly shaped diamonds without holes. Use the sequence of photographs as a reference point for creating the individual triangles and squares.

Base Triangles

Row 1: Insert hook in 2nd ch from hook (on successive triangle, insert hook in next ch), pull up lp (2 lps on hook). Work return pass (see stitch guide).

Row 2: M1 between edge st and first st of previous row, Tss in next vertical bar, insert hook in next ch and pull up lp—4 lps on hook. Work return pass.

Row 3: Tss in next 2 vertical bars, M1 between last vertical bar and selvage edge of previous row. Insert hook in next ch and pull up lp—5 lps on hook. Work return pass.

Row 4: Tss in next 3 vertical bars, M1 between last vertical bar and selvage edge of previous row. Insert

hook in next ch and pull up lp—6 lps on hook. Work return pass.

Row 5: Tss in next 4 vertical bars, M1 between last vertical bar and selvage edge of previous row. Insert hook in next ch and pull up lp—7 lps on hook. Work return pass.

Row 6: Tss in next 5 vertical bars, M1 between last vertical bar and selvage edge of previous row. Insert hook in next ch and pull up lp—8 lps on hook. Work return pass.

Row 7: Sc BO 6 sts, sl st in same ch as last st from previous row (for last triangle, sl st in last free ch)—1 triangle completed.

Work rows 1–7, completing a total of 5 triangles. TURN WORK after last triangle.

Tier 2

Right edge triangle, 4 squares, left edge triangle

Right-Edge Triangle

Row 1: Ch 2, pull up lp in 2nd ch from hook and in stitch at bottom-right corner of last tier—3 lps. Work return pass.

Row 2: M1, Tss in next vertical bar and in edge of last tier's 2nd row—4 lps on hook. Work return pass.

Row 3: M1, Tss in next 2 vertical bars and in edge of last tier's 3rd row—5 lps on hook. Work return pass.

Row 4: M1, Tss in next 3 vertical bars and in edge of last tier's 4th row—6 lps on hook. Work return pass.

Row 5: M1, Tss in next 4 vertical bars and in edge of last tier's 5th row—7 lps on hook. Work return pass.

Row 6: M1, Tss in next 5 vertical bars and in edge of last tier's 6th row—8 lps on hook. Work return pass.

Row 7: Sc BO 6 sts, sl st in next st from last tier—1 lp on hook.

Cont with square.

Square

Row 1: PU 6 sts across bound-off edge of square in last tier, and in first st of next triangle (or subsequent square) in last tier—8 lps on hook. Work return pass.

Rows 2–6: Tss in next 6 vertical bars across row and in edge of last tier's next row. Work return pass. After row 6, there will be 6 rows of vertical bars visible.

Row 7: Sc BO 6 sts, sl st in next st from last tier.

Rep rows 1–7 to make 4 squares.

Cont with left edge triangle.

Left-Edge Triangle

Row 1: PU 6 lps across bound-off row on left side of last tier and in last st of base triangle (or subsequent square)—8 lps on hook. Work return pass.

Row 2: Tss in next 6 vertical bars—7 lps on hook. Work return pass.

Row 3: Tss in next 5 vertical bars—6 lps on hook. Work return pass.

Row 4: Tss in next 4 vertical bars—5 lps on hook. Work return pass.

Row 5: Tss in next 3 vertical bars—4 lps on hook. Work return pass.

Row 6: Tss in next 2 vertical bars—3 lps on hook. Work return pass.

Row 7: Sc BO 1 st—1 lp on hook. TURN WORK.

Tier 3

Work 5 squares, following directions for square in tier 2. TURN WORK after last triangle.

Rep tiers 2 and 3, turning work after each tier, until piece measures 80" or desired length, ending with tier 2. TURN WORK.

End Triangles

Row 1: PU 6 lps across bound-off row of last tier and in first st of next square—8 lps on hook. Work return pass.

Row 2: Sk next vertical bar, Tss in next 5 vertical bars and in edge of last tier's 2nd row—7 lps on hook. Work return pass.

Row 3: Sk next vertical bar, Tss in next 4 vertical bars and in edge of last tier's 3rd row—6 lps on hook. Work return pass.

Row 4: Sk next vertical bar, Tss in next 3 vertical bars and in edge of last tier's 4th row—5 lps on hook. Work return pass.

Row 5: Sk next vertical bar, Tss in next 2 vertical bars and in edge of last tier's 5th row—4 lps on hook. Work return pass.

Row 6: Sk next vertical bar, Tss in next vertical bar and in edge of last tier's 6th row—3 lps on hook. Work return pass.

Row 7: Sk next vertical bar and sl st in next st of last tier—1 lp on hook.

Rep rows 1–7 for a total of 5 end triangles. DO NOT cut yarn.

sangria's SURPRISE

Skill Level: Easy ◼◼◻◻

Finished Measurements: Approx 21" x 66 ", excluding fringe

MATERIALS

7 skeins of ½ N ½ from Kollage (50% milk, 50% wool; 50 g; 174 yds) in color Sangria

Size H-8 (5.0 mm) Tunisian crochet hook or size required for gauge

Size 7 (4.5 mm) crochet hook or one size smaller than Tunisian crochet hook

Gauge: 16 st = 4" in lace patt

Fringe

Before you begin the shawl, cut 112 strands of yarn, 30" long, for fringe. Then work the shawl until only enough yarn is left to BO.

STITCH GUIDE

Foundation forward pass: *Insert hook in next ch, YO and pull up lp, leave lp on hook; rep from * across ch. Do NOT turn work.

Foundation return pass: YO and pull through 1 lp, *YO and pull through 2 lps; rep from * until 1 lp rem.

Tss forward pass: *Insert hook from right to left behind front vertical bar, YO and pull up lp, leave on hook; rep from * across row.

Tss return pass: YO and pull through 1 lp, *YO and pull through 2 lps; rep from * across row until 1 lp rem.

Sl st BO: *Insert hook from right to left behind next front vertical bar, YO and pull through 2 lps on hook; rep from * until sts are bound off.

LACE PATTERN
(Multiple of 2 + 1)

Lace forward pass (row 1): *Insert hook from right to left behind next 2 front vertical bars at same time, YO and pull up lp, leave lp on hook, YO; rep from * across row to last 2 sts, Tss 2.

Lace forward pass (row 2): *Insert hook from right to left behind next front vertical bar, YO and pull up lp, leave lp on hook, insert hook into next ch sp, YO and pull up lp; rep from * across row to last 2 sts, Tss 2.

Lace return pass: Work as for Tss return pass.

SHAWL

With smaller hook, ch 83.

Switch to Tunisian hook. Work foundation forward pass—83 lps on hook. Work foundation return pass.

Work 2 rows of Tss forward and return passes.

Work lace patt as follows:

Row 1: *Work row 1 of lace patt to last 2 sts, end with Tss in next 2 vertical bars. Work return pass.

Row 2: *Work row 2 of lace patt to last 2 sts, end with Tss in next 2 vertical bars. Work return pass.

Rep rows 1 and 2 until piece measures 60", ending with row 2.

Work 2 rows of Tss forward and return passes.

With smaller hook, work sl st BO. Fasten off.

Within this fresh and dazzling shawl—which has a unique stitch pattern, the intense color of sangria, silken drape, and a long fringe—resides a secret. If you hear, "Got Sangria?" astonish everybody with, "Nope, just milk." The yarn is made in part with a milk-protein fiber that is dewatered, then skimmed. Your mother always said milk was good for you, but she never dreamed it could feel so good.

FINISHING

Weave in ends. Block using mist method (see page 77) to smooth and even sts.

Fringe: With 2 strands of fringe held tog, fold in half, making 4 strands in each fringe. Using crochet hook, attach strands of fringe. Insert hook into first st at edge from front to back. Loop strands over hook on back side and pull to front, leaving half the length of strands on back of work. Put 2 fingers through loop and pull ends of strands from back through this loop. Pull firmly to secure. Continue to attach fringe in every 3rd stitch along the edge. *Working from right to left, sk the first 2 strands of the first fringe and use an overhand knot to tie 2 strands from the first fringe with 2 strands from the second fringe about ½" below the first knot where you attached fringe to edge. Cont across the edge, tying 2 strands from one fringe with 2 strands from the next fringe. Tie another row of knots about ½" below the previous row of knots, again tying 2 strands from one fringe with 2 strands from the next fringe. Rep from * once more for 4 rows of knots. Trim ends even.

Milk Casein

Milk-casein protein has been used for centuries as a binder for paints, allowing artists to work with deep, intense colors. To make yarn, the water content is removed, the fat is skimmed off, and then the milk protein fiber is put through a process called wet spinning. The glossy and luxurious appearance gives the look and feel of silk. When blended with wool, the resulting yarn is elegant, comfortable, and warm.

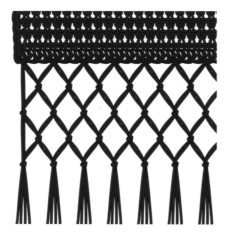

Fringe close-up

Shawl made with two skeins of Malabrigo Sock Yarn in color Archangel

xquisite ALLURE

Skill Level: Easy ◼◼◻◻

Finished Measurements: Approx 50" wide at bottom edge x 16" long, without crochet edge

MATERIALS

Baby Cashmere Merino Silk DK from Sublime (75% extra fine merino, 20% silk, 5% cashmere; 50 g; 116 m/127 yds) 🔵

A 4 skeins in color 161 Lulu

B 2 skeins in color 50 Dilly

Size M/N-13 (9 mm) Tunisian crochet hook with extension or size required to obtain gauge

Size K-10½ (6.5 mm) crochet hook or 2 sizes smaller than Tunisian crochet hook

3 buttons, 1" diameter

Gauge: 12 sts = 4" in patt

STITCH GUIDE

Foundation forward pass: *Insert hook in next ch, YO and pull up lp, leave lp on hook; rep from * across ch. Do NOT turn work.

Foundation return pass: YO and pull through 1 lp, *YO and pull through 2 lps; rep from * until 1 lp rem.

Tss forward pass: *Insert hook from right to left behind front vertical bar, YO and pull up lp, leave lp on hook; rep from * across row.

Tss return pass: YO and pull through 1 lp, *YO and pull through 2 lps; rep from * across row until 1 lp rem.

Sl st BO: *Insert hook from right to left behind front vertical bar, YO and pull through 2 lps on hook; rep from * until sts are bound off.

CROSSED STITCH PATTERN

(Multiple of 2 + 2)

The crossed sts appear one row below the row where sts are crossed.

Row 1: With A, work Tss forward and return passes.

Row 2: With B, work Tss forward and return passes.

Row 3: With A, *sk next vertical bar, Tss into next vertical bar, Tss into skipped vertical bar; rep from * to last st, Tss. Work return pass.

Rep rows 1–3 for patt.

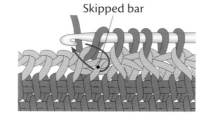

Skipped bar

WRAP

With A and smaller hook, ch 146.

Switch to Tunisian hook. Work foundation forward pass—146 lps on hook. Work foundation return pass.

Work 2 rows of Tss forward and return passes.

Work in crossed st patt until piece measures 10½", ending with row 3.

Next row 1 of patt, dec 8 sts as follows: work 16 sts (17 lps on hook), Tss2tog, work 16 sts, Tss2tog, work 16 sts, Tss2tog, work 10 sts, Tss2tog, work 12 sts, Tss2tog, work 10 sts, Tss2tog, work 16 sts, Tss2tog, work 16 sts, Tss2tog, work 17 sts—138 lps rem.

Work rows 2 and 3 of patt once.

Work rows 1–3 of patt without decs.

Next row 1 of patt, dec 8 sts as follows: work 14 sts (15 lps on hook), Tss2tog, work 14 sts, Tss2tog, work 13 sts, Tss2tog, work 12 sts, Tss2tog, work 14 sts, Tss2tog, work 12 sts, Tss2tog, work 14 sts, Tss2tog, work 13 sts, Tss2tog, work 15 sts—130 sts rem.

Work rows 2 and 3 of patt once.

Work rows 1–3 of patt without decs.

Next row 1 of patt, dec 5 sts as follows: work 49 sts (50 sts on hook), Tss2tog, work 6 sts, Tss2tog, work 4 sts, Tss2tog, work 4 sts, Tss2tog, work 6 sts, Tss2tog, work 50 sts—125 lps rem.

*Whether you're enjoying
a morning cup of joe
on the veranda or an
evening out on the town,
this sublime striped wrap
with subtle X-stitch detail
will keep the chill off your
shoulders. The shoulder
shaping and angular
closure keep the wrap in
place. This exquisite
wrap is perfect for
any occasion.*

With A, work 2 rows of Tss forward and return passes.

With smaller hook, sl st BO. Do not cut yarn.

FINISHING

Cont with smaller hook and A, work edging as follows:

Rnd 1: Sc around all edges, working 3 sc into each corner st, sl st to join.

Mark placement for buttonholes approximately 1½", 4½", and 7½" from corner join along top edge. Adjust to fit your body size.

Rnd 2: With B, ch 1, *with B, sk 1 st, work sc into next st, sc in skipped st; rep from * around all edges. Make buttonholes as follows: *at marker, ch 2, sk 2 sc from previous row, cont to next marker; rep from * to end of rnd, sl st to join.

Rnd 3: With A, sc around all edges, working 2 sc into each corner st. Do not join; fasten off and join with duplicate st (see page 75).

Weave in ends. Sew buttons along short edge that is farthest from buttonholes to correspond with buttonholes. Block with mist method (see page 77) to smooth and even sts.

Option

For a more-typical rectangle wrap, omit decs and finish as directed, omitting buttonholes.

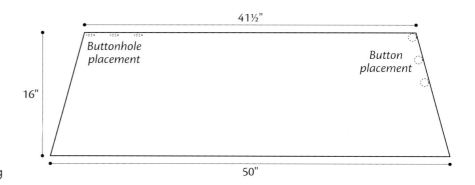

41½"

16"

Buttonhole placement

Button placement

50"

Front

Back

⤳ essential PLEASURE ⤳

Skill Level: Easy ◼◼◻◻

Finished Measurements: 39" x 57"

MATERIALS

A 10 skeins of Worsted Merino Superwash from Plymouth Yarn (100% superwash fine merino wool; 100 g; 218 yds) in color 27 ◼4◼

B 2 skeins of Boucle Merino Superwash from Plymouth Yarn (90% superwash fine merino wool, 10% nylon; 100 g; 235 yds) in color 27 ◼4◼

Size O-17 (12 mm) Tunisian crochet hook with extension or size required to obtain gauge

Size N/P-15 (10 mm) crochet hook or one size smaller than Tunisian crochet hook

DVD movie case, piece of plastic, or sturdy cardboard for tassel making

Gauge: 10 sts = 4" in patt Chevron st with 2 strands of A held tog throughout

STITCH GUIDE

Foundation forward pass: *Insert hook in next ch, YO and pull up lp, leave lp on hook; rep from * across ch. Do NOT turn work.

Foundation return pass: YO and pull through 1 lp, *YO and pull through 2 lps; rep from * until 1 lp rem.

Tss forward pass: *Insert hook from right to left behind front vertical bar, YO and pull up lp, leave lp on hook; rep from * across row.

Tss return pass: YO and pull through 1 lp, *YO and pull through 2 lps; rep from * across row until 1 lp rem.

M1: Insert hook in sp between lp on hook and next vertical bar, YO and pull up lp.

Tss3tog: Working left to right, insert hook behind next 3 vertical bars, YO and pull up lp.

Sl st BO: Omitting incs and decs, *insert hook from right to left behind front vertical bar, YO and pull through 2 lps on hook; rep from * until sts are bound off.

CHEVRON PATTERN

(Multiple of 14 + 1)

Every forward pass: With 2 strands of A held together, *M1, Tss 5, Tss3tog, Tss 5, M1, Tss; rep from * across row.

Return pass: Work as for Tss return pass.

AFGHAN

With smaller crochet hook and 2 strands of A held tog, ch 99.

Switch to Tunisian hook. Work foundation forward pass—99 lps on hook. Work foundation return pass.

Work in chevron patt until piece measures 57".

Work sl st BO. Fasten off.

Impressive, indulgent, indispensable. Whatever terms you use to describe this iconic chevron afghan with oversized and ever-so-slightly unruly tassels, you know it is an "essential pleasure" that you don't want to do without. Better yet, the superwash wool means it's easy care, so you can indulge every day.

FINISHING

With RS facing, larger crochet hook, and 2 strands of B held tog, sc around all sides, working 3 sc into each corner and at the point of each chevron. Fasten off and join with duplicate st (see page 75). Weave in all ends. Block using mist method (see page 77).

Tassels (make 15)

Cut 2 strands of A approximately 16" long. Use a DVD movie case, piece of plastic, or sturdy cardboard that is approx 7½" x 5¼" for a frame. Wrap a single strand of B around the 7½" length of the frame 55 times. Cut B. Insert a double strand of A under the strands on top of tassel and knot tightly. Slip tassel off frame. Cut open bottom loops. With a second strand of A folded in half, wrap around tassel about 1½" from top and knot securely. Rep for a total of 15 tassels. Attach a tassel to each chevron point. Trim ends as needed.

Oversized tassels

TRANQUIL Escape

Skill Level: Intermediate ◼◼◼◻

Sizes: Small (Medium, Large, Extra Large)

Finished Bust Measurement: 38½ (41, 44, 46½)"

Finished Back Length: 23 (24, 25, 26)"

MATERIALS

3 (4, 4, 5) skeins of Pima Cotton/ Silk from Misti Alpaca (83% Peruvian pima cotton, 17% silk; 100 g; 327 yds/300 m) in color 636 Berry Wine ❸

Size H-8 (5 mm) Tunisian crochet hook or size required to obtain gauge

Size G-6 (4 mm) crochet hook or one size smaller than Tunisian crochet hook

3 buttons, ⅜" (9 mm) diameter

Gauge: 18 sts = 4" in patt

Notes

Garment is worked in three pieces: back and two fronts. Sleeves are made by casting on additional stitches at the underarm.

Return pass of lace pattern is different from standard return. See lace pattern return pass below right.

STITCH GUIDE

Foundation forward pass: *Insert hook in next ch, YO and pull up lp, leave lp on hook; rep from * across ch. Do NOT turn work.

Foundation return pass: YO and pull through 1 lp, (YO and pull through 2 lps) twice, *ch 1, YO, pull through 4 lps, ch 1, (YO and pull through 2 lps) 3 times; rep from * until 1 lp rem.

Tss forward pass: *Insert hook from right to left behind front vertical bar, YO and pull up lp, leave lp on hook; rep from * across row.

Tss return pass: YO and pull through 1 lp, *YO and pull through 2 lps; rep from * across row until 1 lp rem.

Tss2tog: Insert hook from right to left behind next 2 vertical bars tog, YO and pull up lp.

Sl st BO: *Insert hook from right to left behind front vertical bar, YO and pull through 2 lps on hook; rep from * until sts are bound off.

LACE PATTERN

(Multiple of 6 + 3)

Lace forward pass: Tss in next 2 vertical bars (3 lps on hook), *insert hook under next ch sp, YO and pull up lp, leave lp on hook, insert hook into ch lp over center cluster on previous row, YO and pull up lp, leave lp on hook, insert hook under next ch sp, YO and pull up lp, leave lp on hook, Tss into next 3 sts; rep from * across row.

Lace return pass: YO and pull through 1 lp, (YO and pull through 2 lps) twice, *ch 1, YO and pull through 4 lps, ch 1, (YO and pull through 2 lps) 3 times; rep from * until 1 lp rem.

Escape to the East in this flowing kimono-inspired cardigan with short sleeves and a simple pearl-button closure. The rhythmic lace-shell pattern is relaxing to work and produces an upscale, graceful drape. No need to save this for special occasions; enjoy a tranquil escape every time you slip into this cardigan.

BACK

With smaller hook, ch 87 (93, 99, 105).

Switch to Tunisian crochet hook. Work foundation forward pass—87 (93, 99, 105) lps on hook. Work foundation return pass.

Work in patt st until piece measures 14 (15, 16, 17)".

Change to Tss as follows: Work lace forward pass. Work Tss return pass.

Work 1 row of Tss forward and return passes.

Inc for sleeves as follows: Ch 12, work foundation forward pass in each ch (12 lps on hook), cont across row in Tss—99 (105, 111, 117) lps on hook. With separate piece of yarn, ch 12, work foundation forward pass in each ch—111 (117, 123, 129) lps on hook.

Cont in Tss until piece measures 23 (24, 25, 26)".

With smaller hook, sl st BO.

LEFT FRONT

With smaller hook, ch 45 (51, 51, 57).

Switch to Tunisian crochet hook. Work foundation forward pass—45 (51, 51, 57) lps on hook. Work foundation return pass.

Work in lace patt until piece measures 14 (15, 16, 17)".

Back

Change to Tss as follows: Work lace forward pass. Work Tss return pass.

Work 1 row of Tss forward and return passes.

Inc for sleeves as follows: Ch 12, work foundation forward pass in each ch—12 lps on hook, cont across row in Tss—57 (63, 63, 69) lps on hook.

Cont in Tss until piece measures 19 (20, 21, 22)".

Cont in Tss, shape neck as follows: Work forward pass until 49 (55, 55, 61) lps rem on hook, leave 8 bars unworked, work return pass. Work forward pass until 44 (50, 50, 56) lps rem on hook, leave 5 sts unworked. Work return pass. Work forward pass to last 3 sts, Tss2tog,

Tss in last st—43 (49, 49, 55) lps on hook. Work return pass. Work forward pass to last 3 sts, Tss2tog, Tss in last st—42 (48, 48, 54) lps on hook. Work return pass.

Cont in Tss until piece measures 23 (24, 25, 26)".

With smaller hook, sl st BO.

RIGHT FRONT

With smaller hook, ch 45 (51, 51, 57).

Switch to Tunisian crochet hook. Work foundation forward pass—45 (51, 51, 57) lps on hook. Work foundation return pass.

Work in lace patt until piece measures 14 (15, 16, 17)".

Change to Tss as follows: Work lace forward pass. Work Tss return pass.

Work 1 row of Tss forward and return passes.

Inc for sleeves as follows: Work Tss forward pass; with separate piece of yarn, ch 12, work foundation forward pass in each ch—57 (63, 63, 69) lps on hook. Work Tss return pass.

Cont Tss until piece measures 19 (20, 21, 22)".

Shape neck as follows: Sl st BO next 8 sts, Tss across row—49 (55, 55, 61) lps on hook. Work Tss return pass. Sl st BO next 5 sts, Tss across row—44 (50, 50, 56) lps on hook. Work Tss return pass. Tss2tog, Tss to end of row—43 (49, 49, 55) loops on hook. Work Tss return pass. Tss2tog, Tss to end of row—42 (48, 48, 54) lps on hook.

Cont in Tss until piece measures 23 (24, 25, 26)".

With smaller hook, sl st BO.

FINISHING

With RS tog, sl-st crochet (page 75) shoulders, underarm and side seams tog. With smaller hook and RS facing, beg at underarm seam, sc along entire edge, working 3 sc into each corner st, join with sl st and ch 2. Dc in each sc of previous row, working 3 dc into each corner st. Fasten off and join with duplicate st (see page 75). Position buttons on left front and sew in place. Buttons will slip through dcs. Block using mist method (see page 77) to smooth and even sts.

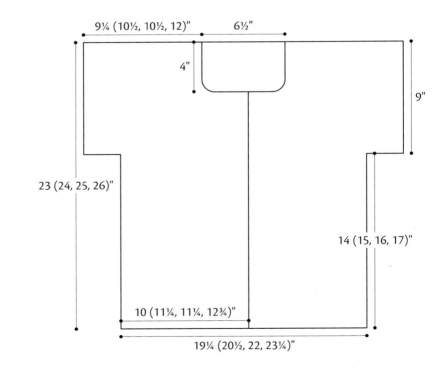

9¼ (10½, 10½, 12)"   6½"

4"

9"

23 (24, 25, 26)"

14 (15, 16, 17)"

10 (11¼, 11¼, 12¾)"

19¼ (20½, 22, 23¼)"

~ LOVELY existence ~

Skill Level: Intermediate ◼◼◼◻

Sizes: Small (Medium, Large, Extra Large)

Finished Bust Measurement: 38 (42, 44, 46)"

Finished Length at Shoulder: 18 (19½, 21¼, 23½)"

MATERIALS

Zara from Filatura Di Crosa (100% extra fine merino superwash; 50 g/1.75 oz; 136 yds/125 m) 🧶

A 2 skeins in color 1481 Denim

B 2 skeins in color 1798 Seafoam Green

C 6 (7, 8, 9) skeins in color 1796 Light Spring Green

Size I-9 (5.5 mm) Tunisian crochet hook or size required to obtain gauge

Size H-8 (5 mm) crochet hook or one size smaller than Tunisian crochet hook

Gauge: 4.5 st = 1" in patt

Consider working the hand warmers as a gauge swatch.

STITCH GUIDE

Foundation forward pass: *Insert hook in next ch, YO and pull up lp, leave lp on hook; rep from * across ch. Do NOT turn work.

Foundation return pass: YO and pull through 1 lp, *YO and pull through 2 lps; rep from * until 1 lp rem.

Sc BO: *Insert hook from right to left behind front vertical bar, YO and pull up lp, YO and pull through 2 lps on hook; rep from * across until sts are bound off (see page 46).

EYELET PATTERN

(Multiple of 6 + 3)

Eyelet forward pass: Tss 2 (3 lps on hook), *YO, sk next vertical bar, Tss in next vertical bar, YO, sk next vertical bar, Tss in next 3 vertical bars; rep from * across row.

Eyelet return pass: YO and pull through 1 lp, *YO and pull through 2 lps; rep from * across row until 1 lp rem.

PULLOVER

Front and back are worked in one piece from left cuff, across body, ending with right cuff.

Color changes are done at right edge when 2 loops remain on hook (see page 18).

With smaller hook and A, ch 69 (69, 75, 81).

Switch to Tunisian crochet hook. Work foundation forward pass—69 (69, 75, 81) lps on hook. Work foundation return pass.

Working in eyelet patt, work color sequence as follows:

   9 rows of A

   1 row of C

   5 rows of A

   1 row of C

   3 rows of A

   (1 row of C, 1 row of A) 3 times

   5 rows of C

Cont with C, at end of return pass, ch 48 (54, 60, 66) for body, work foundation forward pass on new chs, then cont with eyelett patt to end.

At end of forward pass, with separate piece of yarn, ch 48 (54, 60, 66) for body, remove hook from ch and return to beg of ch, work foundation forward pass on new chs to left edge—165 (177, 195, 213) lps on hook. Work Tss return pass.

Cont in established patt until body measures 4½ (5½, 6, 6½)".

Shape neck opening as follows: Work 78 (84, 93, 102) lps on hook, sl st next 9 sts, cont in patt over last 78 (84, 93, 102) lps, work return pass to neck edge. Enlarge last lp and remove from hook, attach second ball of yarn and cont with

At first glance it seems basic: a simple tee, a nice first impression. With another glance you realize there is considerably more panache. The shorter, different-colored sleeves; the clean lines of banded pattern stitch; and the classic bateau neck transition this simple tee with coordinating hand warmers into a lovely way of life. And if you have beautiful bracelets, leave the hand warmers at home and sport your bracelets instead.

return pass. Working front and back at same time, using one ball of yarn for front and another for back, and moving hook from front to back at neck edge, cont until body measures 14½ (15½, 16, 16½)".

Join front and back as follows: Work forward pass as established, work return pass to neck edge, ch 9, and cont across pass with same ball of yarn. On next forward pass, work 9 chs as foundation forward pass. Cont until piece measures 19 (21, 22, 23)".

Shape second sleeve as follows: Sl st 48 (54, 60, 66) sts, cont in patt over 69 (69, 75, 81) sts, leave last

48 (54, 60, 66) sts unworked. Work return pass. Work color sequence as follows:

> 9 rows of C
>
> (1 row of B, 1 row of C) 3 times
>
> 3 rows of B
>
> 1 row of C
>
> 5 rows of B
>
> 1 row of C
>
> 7 rows of B

With smaller hook and B, sc BO.

FINISHING

With RS tog, sl-st crochet (page 75) side and underarm seams tog. With smaller hook and C, beg at one corner, sc along neck edge. Fasten off st and join with duplicate st (see page 75). With smaller hook and C, beg at side seam, sc along bottom edge. Fasten off st and join with duplicate st. With smaller hook and appropriate color, sc along each cuff. Block using pin-and-mist method (see page 77) to smooth and even sts.

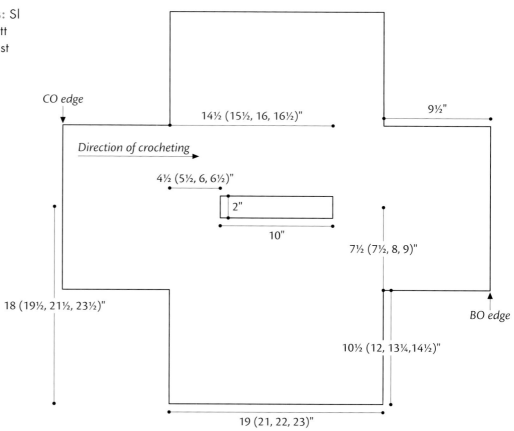

CO edge

14½ (15½, 16, 16½)"

9½"

Direction of crocheting

4½ (5½, 6, 6½)"

2"

10"

7½ (7½, 8, 9)"

BO edge

18 (19½, 21½, 23½)"

10½ (12, 13¼, 14½)"

19 (21, 22, 23)"

HAND WARMERS (MAKE 2)

With smaller hook and A, ch 33.

Switch to Tunisian crochet hook. Work basic foundation forward pass—33 lps on hook. Work foundation return pass.

Work in patt st until piece measures 7½". Work sl st BO (see page 15).

With RS tog, fold piece in half with side edges aligned. Sl-st crochet (page 75) sides tog for 4", leave 1½" opening for thumb, finish 2" seam.

Rep for second hand warmer using B.

❧ free SPIRIT ❧

Skill Level: Intermediate ◼◼◼◻

Sizes: Small (Medium, Large, Extra Large)

Finished Bust Measurement: 38 (42, 44, 48)" when buttoned

Finished Back Length: 22 (23½, 24½, 25¼)"

MATERIALS

6 (7, 8, 8) skeins of Free Spirit from Trendsetter Yarns (62% cotton, 13% acrylic, 13% linen, 12% nylon; 100 g/3.5 oz; 175 yds) in color 5 ◢4◣

Size I-9 (5.5 mm) Tunisian crochet hook with extension or size required to obtain gauge

Size H-8 (5 mm) crochet hook or one size smaller than Tunisian crochet hook

1 button, 1½" diameter

Gauge: 11 sts and 7 rows = 4" in patt

STITCH GUIDE

Foundation forward pass: *Insert hook in next ch, YO and pull up lp, leave lp on hook; rep from * across ch. Do NOT turn work.

Foundation return pass: YO and pull through 1 lp, *YO and pull through 2 lps; rep from *, until 1 lp rem.

Sc BO: *Insert hook from right to left behind front vertical bar, YO and pull up lp, YO and pull through 2 lps on hook; rep from * across until sts are bound off (see page 46).

Inc row: Skipping first st as usual, insert hook into sp before next vertical bar, YO and pull up lp, YO and pull through 1 lp—first inc made. Work in patt to last st, insert hook into sp before last vertical bar, YO and pull up lp, YO and pull through 1 lp—second inc made.

Dec row: Skipping first st as usual, insert hook into next 2 vertical bars as for a Tks, YO and pull up lp, YO and pull through 1 lp—first dec made. Work in patt to last 3 sts, insert hook into 2 vertical bars as for a Tks, YO and pull up lp, YO and pull through 1 lp—second dec made.

CORDED PATTERN

Corded forward pass: Working right to left, ch 1, *insert hook through next vertical bar from front to back as if to knit, YO and pull up lp, YO and pull through 1 lp; rep from * across row.

Corded return pass: YO and pull through 1 lp, *YO and pull through 2 lps; rep from * until 1 lp rem.

Corded sl st BO: Ch 1, *insert hook through next vertical bar from front to back as if to knit, YO and pull up lp, YO and pull through 2 lps; rep from * until sts are bound off.

JACKET

Jacket starts at right cuff and is worked from side to side. The left front is worked separately and then joined to the back before working left sleeve and ending with left cuff. The width of the combined left and right fronts is greater than the width of the back. This allows for a more relaxed fit.

Right Sleeve

With smaller hook, ch 32 (32, 34, 34).

The flattering and slenderizing vertical lines of the stitch pattern with interspersed whips of color and the relaxed fit of this unstructured, single-buttoned jacket will free your spirit. Feel confident enough to wander the world in this jacket, which is worked from cuff to cuff with minimal shaping, folded lapels, and crochet edges.

Switch to Tunisian crochet hook. Work foundation forward pass—32 (32, 34, 34) lps on hook. Work foundation return pass.

Work 2 rows in corded patt.

Work inc row.

Cont in patt, working inc row every 3 rows 8 (8, 9, 9) more times—50 (50, 54, 54) lps on hook.

Work 3 (3, 1, 1) more row(s) in patt for a total of 30 (30, 31, 31) rows, ending with return pass.

Body

At end of return pass, ch 36 (40, 42, 44) for body, work foundation forward pass on new chs, then cont corded forward pass to end.

At end of forward pass, with separate piece of yarn, ch 36 (40, 42, 44) for body, remove hook from ch and return to beg of ch, work foundation forward pass on new chs to left edge—122 (130, 138, 142) lps on hook. Work return pass.

Cont in patt until body measures 5½ (6½, 7, 8)".

Right Front

Work first 61 (65, 69, 71) sts in patt, leaving rem sts unworked.

Cont in patt until right front measures 11½ (12½, 13, 14)".

Work corded sl st BO. Cut yarn.

Back

With RS facing, attach yarn at right front neck edge and work 61 (65, 69, 71) sts in patt.

Cont in patt until back measures 13½ (14½, 15, 16)".

At end of return pass, remove hook from rem lp and set piece aside.

Left Front (worked separately)

With smaller hook, ch 61 (65, 69, 71).

Switch to Tunisian crochet hook. Work foundation forward pass—61 (65, 69, 71) lps on hook. Work foundation return pass.

Cont in patt until piece measures 6", ending with return pass.

Joining Left Front to Back

Work 61 (65, 69, 71) sts of left front. With RS of back facing, join by cont in patt across row—122 (130, 138, 142) lps on hook.

Cont in patt until back measures 19 (21, 22, 24)".

Left Sleeve

Working corded sl st, BO 36 (40, 42, 44) sts, work in patt over next 50 (50, 54, 54) sts, leave rem 36 (40, 42, 44) sts unworked.

Work 3 (3, 1, 1) rows in corded patt.

Work dec row.

Cont in patt, working dec row every 3 rows 8 (8, 9, 9) more times for a total of 30 (30, 31, 31) rows, ending with return pass—32 (32, 34, 34) sts.

Work corded sl st BO over 32 (32, 34, 34) sts.

FINISHING

With RS tog, st-st crochet (page 75) underarm and side seams tog. Mark placement for buttonhole, approx 7" (or desired length) from bottom edge. With smaller hook and RS facing, beg at side seam, sc along entire edge. Join with sl st and work 1 row of reverse sc around entire edge, working buttonhole as follows: ch 4, sk 4 sc from previous row, cont reverse sc to end of round. Fasten off yarn and join with duplicate st (see page 75). Sc around cuff opening.

Determine button placement, adjusting for desired personal fit and sew button in place. For a more relaxed look, leave the button off and allow the fronts to drape open. Weave in all ends. Block with mist method (see page 77) to smooth and even sts.

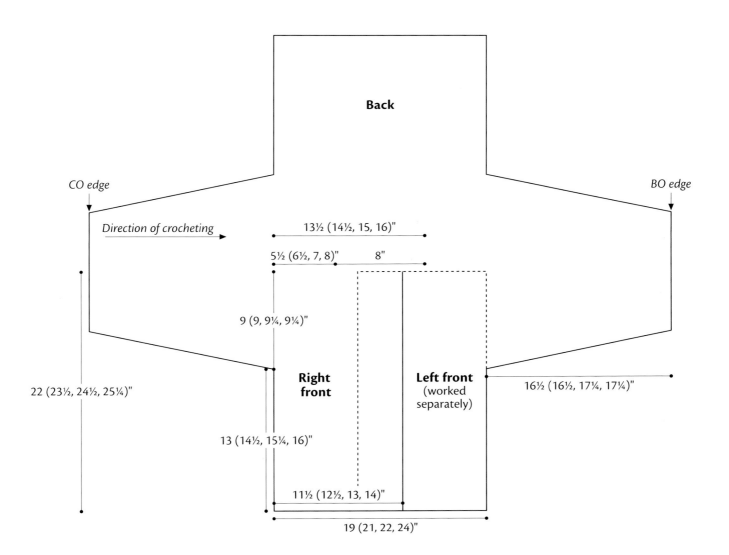

Back

CO edge

BO edge

Direction of crocheting

13½ (14½, 15, 16)"

5½ (6½, 7, 8)"　　8"

9 (9, 9¼, 9¼)"

Right front

Left front
(worked separately)

16½ (16½, 17¼, 17¼)"

22 (23½, 24½, 25¼)"

13 (14½, 15¼, 16)"

11½ (12½, 13, 14)"

19 (21, 22, 24)"

abbreviations

approx	approximately		RS	right side
beg	begin(ning)		sc	single crochet
BO	bind off		sk	skip
ch(s)	chain(s)		sl st	slip stitch
CO	cast on		sp	space
cont	continue, continuing		st(s)	stitch(es)
dec(s)	decrease(s)		tog	together
dc	double crochet		Tks	Tunisian knit stitch
hdc	half double crochet		Tps	Tunisian purl stitch
inc(s)	increase(s)		Tss	Tunisian simple stitch
lp(s)	loop(s)		Tss2tog	work 2 stitches together—1 stitch decreased (see page 17)
m	meters			
M1	make 1 stitch—1 stitch increased (see page 16)		Tss3tog	work 3 stitches together—2 stitches decreased (see page 17)
patt	pattern			
PU	pick up		WS	wrong side
rem	remain(s)(ing)		yd(s)	yard(s)
rep	repeat		YO	yarn over
rnd	round			

TECHNIQUES for an attractive finish

Good finishing makes the difference between a professional, tailored-looking piece of work and one that looks homemade. Here are some of the basic techniques necessary to give your work a fine tailored look.

JOINING A NEW BALL OF YARN

A great finish begins long before the end is in sight. Whenever possible, attach a new ball of yarn at the beginning of the row. Place the end of the yarn over the hook and begin to work. If you prefer to anchor your yarn, tie the new strand onto the old tail with a single knot. Slide the new knot up the old tail to the hook and begin working with the new yarn.

JOINING WITH DUPLICATE STITCH

Based on the duplicate stitch used in knitting, this method gives a smooth join. After working the final round, fasten off the stitch and thread the

tail through a tapestry needle. Insert the needle from front to back under the back leg of the round's last stitch, covering the first stitch of the round. Weave the tail into the back of the work.

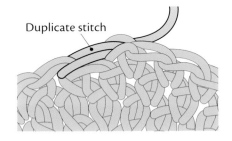

Duplicate stitch

SEAMING

A few of the projects require seaming and there are several methods suited to Tunisian crochet. Regardless of the method you prefer, seams should be smooth and not easily detected.

Whipstitch gives a flat, durable seam. Align edges with the right sides together and wrong sides facing out. Using a tapestry needle, take needle from front

to back through both layers of fabric, keeping the front and back corresponding stitches together. Repeat across edge.

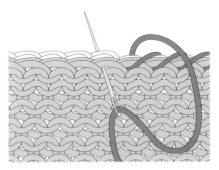

Slip-stitch crochet gives a flexible, yet stable seam. Align edges with right sides together for an inside ridge, or wrong sides together for an outside ridge. Use the same size crochet hook you used to make the beginning chain. Insert hook through stitch on both layers, yarn over hook and pull through both layers and through loop on hook. Repeat across edge.

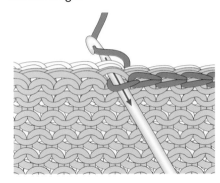

CROCHETING EDGES

Tunisian crochet usually requires a crochet edge to help the edges lie flat and give the piece a better finish. Generally a smaller hook size is used for the edge than the size used for the body of the work. A round of single crochet (sc) is worked as the first round and serves as a foundation for additional rounds. When you're working into a corner stitch, you can work two or three stitches into the same stitch to create the curve of the corner. A crochet edge is also an easy way to create buttonhole loops.

Single Crochet (sc)

To work, insert the hook into the stitch, yarn over the hook and pull up a loop (two loops on hook), yarn over the hook and pull through both loops.

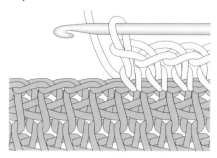

Half Double Crochet (hdc)

To work, yarn over the hook, insert the hook into the stitch, yarn over the hook and pull up a loop (three loops on hook), yarn over the hook and pull through all three loops.

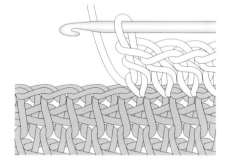

Double Crochet (dc)

To work, yarn over the hook, insert the hook into the stitch, yarn over the hook and pull up a loop (three loops on hook), yarn over the hook and pull through two loops (two loops remaining), yarn over the hook and pull through both loops.

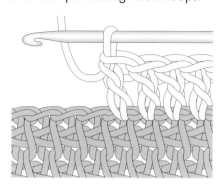

Reverse Single Crochet

Also known as shrimp or crab stitch, this stitch is a single crochet worked in reverse—that is, from left to right instead of from right to left. To work, insert hook into next stitch on the right, yarn over the hook and pull up a loop (two loops on hook), yarn over the hook and pull through both loops.

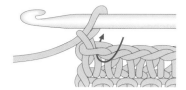

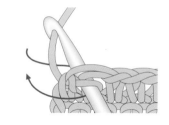

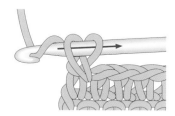

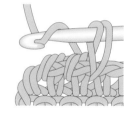

WORKING A BUTTONHOLE LOOP

To work a buttonhole loop, skip the required number of stitches and work the same number of chains. On successive rounds, work a single crochet into each chain.

WEAVING IN ENDS

Thread a tapestry needle and weave the yarn through three or four stitches on the wrong side of the work. Check the right side to be sure the stitches are not showing before clipping yarn.

BLOCKING

First choose a flat, waterproof surface to spread out the piece you're blocking. You can purchase a blocking board, use the top of an ironing board for smaller pieces, or cover the floor with a towel. Regardless of the method used for blocking, the piece should remain in place until dry.

Mist Method

Lay the knitted piece on the surface, shaping it to specified dimensions. Fill a clean spray bottle with water and mist lightly with water. Allow to dry completely before moving.

Pin-and-Mist Method

Lay the knitted piece on the surface. Pin piece to specified measurements. Fill a clean spray bottle with water and mist heavily with water. Allow to dry completely before removing pins.

Wet Blocking Method

Dip knitted piece in cool water. Gently squeeze out the water. *Do not wring or twist piece.* Roll piece in an absorbent bath towel to blot out the excess water. Spread on a flat surface and pin to specified dimensions. Allow to dry completely before removing pins.

~ USEFUL information ~

STANDARD YARN WEIGHTS						
Yarn-Weight Symbol and Category Name	**1** Super Fine	**2** Fine	**3** Light	**4** Medium	**5** Bulky	**6** Super Bulky
Types of Yarn in Category	Sock, Fingering, Baby	Sport, Baby	DK, Light Worsted	Worsted, Afghan, Aran	Chunky, Craft, Rug	Bulky, Roving
Crochet Gauge* Range in Single Crochet to 4"	21 to 32 sts	16 to 20 sts	12 to 17 sts	11 to 14 sts	8 to 11 sts	5 to 9 sts
Recommended Hook in Metric Size Range	2.25 to 3.5 mm	3.5 to 4.5 mm	4.5 to 5.5 mm	5.5 to 6.5 mm	6.5 to 9 mm	9 mm and larger
Recommended Hook in U.S. Size Range	B-1 to E-4	E-4 to 7	7 to I-9	I-9 to K-10½	K-10½ to M-13	M-13 and larger

These are guidelines only. The above reflect the most commonly used gauges and hook sizes for specific yarn categories.

METRIC CONVERSIONS

Yards x .91 = meters
Meters x 1.09 = yards
Grams x .035 = ounces
Ounces x 28.35 = grams

SKILL LEVELS

■□□□ **Beginner:** Projects for first-time crocheters using basic stitches; minimal shaping.

■■□□ **Easy:** Projects using yarn with basic stitches, repetitive stitch patterns, simple color changes, and simple shaping and finishing.

■■■□ **Intermediate:** Projects using a variety of techniques, such as basic lace patterns or color patterns; midlevel shaping and finishing.

■■■■ **Experienced:** Projects with intricate stitch patterns, techniques, and dimension, such as nonrepeating patterns, multicolor techniques, fine threads, small hooks, detailed shaping, and refined finishing.

CROCHET HOOK SIZES

Tunisian hooks are available in the following sizes.

Millimeter	U.S. Size*
3.75 mm	F-5
4 mm	G-6
4.5 mm	7
5 mm	H-8
5.5 mm	I-9
6 mm	J-10
6.5 mm	K-10½
8 mm	L-11
9 mm	M/N-13
10 mm	N/P-15
12 mm	O-17
15 mm	P/Q
16 mm	Q-19
19 mm	S-35
22 mm	T-42
25 mm	U-50

*Letter or number may vary. Rely on the millimeter sizing.

RESOURCES

Contact the following companies to locate the yarns and supplies used in this book.

Berroco Yarns
www.berroco.com
Bonsai

Denise Interchangeable Crochet Hooks
www.knitdenise.com

Dream in Color
www.dreamincoloryarn.com
Smooshy

Filatura Di Crosa
www.tahkistacycharles.com
Zara

Great Adirondack Yarn Co.
Gossamer

Knit One Crochet Too
www.knitonecrochettoo.com
Linus

Kollage
www.kollageyarns.com
½ N ½

Manos del Uruguay
www.fairmountfibers.com
Wool Classica

Misti Alpaca
www.mistialpaca.com
Pima cotton/silk

Nashua Knits
www.nashuaknits.com
Creative Focus Linen

Noro
www.knittingfever.com
Silk Garden

Plymouth Yarns
www.plymouthyarn.com
Fantasy Naturale
Grass
Worsted Merino Superwash
Boucle Merino Superwash

Rowan Yarns
www.westminsterfibers.com
Summer Tweed

Sublime
www.knittingfever.com
Baby Cashmere Merino Silk DK

Trendsetter Yarns
www.trendsetteryarns.com
Free Spirit

You might also enjoy these other fine titles from Martingale & Company

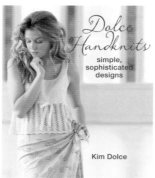

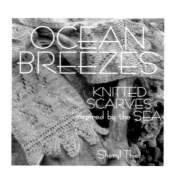

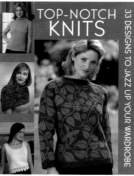